When Love & Sorrow Embrace

The Sufficiency of God's Grace
Through the Heartache of Miscarriage

By

Beth Forbus, MA

Sarah's Laughter
Christian Support for Infertility & Child Loss
www.Sarahs-Laughter.com
A division of Shepherd Ministries

In anticipation of a glorious reunion with the babies
you have loved and lost,
this work is dedicated to all who have found themselves
in the embrace of love and sorrow.

Table of Contents

Acknowledgements

To my Heavenly Father. I thank You from the very depths of my being for loving me. I cannot imagine why You've chosen to use me, but I am forever grateful.

To my husband, Jason. Without you, Sarah's Laughter would not exist. Thank you for supporting me throughout my various "projects".

To my miracle, Lexie. God must have such marvelous plans for you! I cannot wait to watch His plan unfold in your life! I'm so proud to be your mom!

To Shepherd Ministries. Thank you for your constant support to me in the ministry of Sarah's Laughter. Your support has made it possible for me to reach out to a silently suffering community with the comfort of the Word of God.

Foreword

〰〰

Over the years, I have been called upon in many cases, to stand with grieving families in their darkest hours of grief. I confess, as a Pastor, I probably wasn't aware of the depth of hurt, confusion and frustration that a couple faces in the loss of an unborn or stillborn baby. I have always been ready to reach out and to "be there" for those with any kind of a problem to help where I could. However, I found myself at a loss as to how to help someone suffering a miscarriage. I wish I'd had *When Love & Sorrow Embrace* to give to every family that had lost their precious baby. Every pastor and counselor should have this book in his or her library.

When a couple miscarries their baby, they grieve in different ways. Some grit their teeth and endure, while some even curse God. In *When Love & Sorrow Embrace*, author Beth Forbus has the unique writer's ability to make the Word of God simply come alive! She approaches the difficult questions plaguing the grieving parents, and answers directly from the Word of God to give encouraging help to readers. This book approaches child loss and miscarriage with rock-solid, Biblical and eternal encouragement for all who have suffered miscarriage. The reader will truly know and experience God's love. We are never exempt from trials but through trials we are made more aware of His Grace. When all else fails in the complexities of life, God always comes through. Only through Christ can we cease to be victims and become victors instead.

When you read Beth's presentation of David and Goliath or the story of your Savior sleeping during the storm, you'll feel as if you actually lived in those days. You'll find that the three Hebrew children were not alone in the fiery furnace, and that God let Goliath fall face down to show who the victor really was. You'll even find encouragement to help you through your loss in the story of Peter walking on the water, and Mary pouring her oil on Jesus' feet. The wonderful Word of God comes alive as you learn about God's knowledge and personal acquaintance with your baby, in or out of the womb. You'll find that God has great love for the miscarried baby as well as for both parents. God's Word is precious and eternal, and holds the answer for you in this difficult time of your life.

The Word of God, which is made so clear and meaningful in *When Love & Sorrow Embrace* can be applied to various situations of sorrow, trials and life's complications. How else could God know how much we love Him, if we never had a trial or a problem? Heaven is waiting, and those preceding your arrival will only make Heaven sweeter.

Beth Barker Forbus is my third daughter and I thank God very humbly for her ministry, Sarah's Laughter, Christian Support for Infertility & Child Loss. May all who read this book be richly blessed and brought into the spiritual realm of divine encouragement.

Paul F. Barker, Th.G
Founder
Shepherd Ministries

Just a moment of your time before you begin...

If you are holding this book in your hands, there's a good chance that your eyes are clouded by tears and your broken heart is trying its best to mend. Your life has been irreversibly changed by the baby-shaped void in your life since the moment you realized you had lost your precious baby to miscarriage. Perhaps you held your baby in your arms for only a few moments, trying to memorize every feature and every detail before the nurses took him or her away. Maybe the only place you've ever seen your child's face was in your dreams as you held a positive pregnancy test in your hands. Your arms literally ache to hold your baby, yet you find yourself holding a book on miscarriage instead. Whatever the case may be, you have suffered a devastating loss that many experience but few understand. Surely life has no greater sorrow than the death of a baby, whether born or unborn. However, we serve a mighty God whose grace is sufficient to bring you through such a heartache with greater vision and purpose than you ever could have dreamed!

Throughout Scripture we see people just like you and me who have experienced all the joys and sorrows that life brings. We see marriages and we see divorces. We see joy and we see sorrow. We see families expanding and we see them dwindling. It is no mistake that the Giver of Life included stories of grief within His living Word. If you feel alone in your struggle to survive the loss of your baby, take heart! You'll find understanding written within the pages of the Bible.

When you cry out to God and feel as though your prayers are pounding on the closed doors of Heaven, perhaps you feel like David felt. You have a day where it feels as if life is returning to normal, only to suddenly crumple beneath the weight of an empty cradle. Peter could understand. You find yourself wondering why God didn't show up when you needed Him the most, and you have just joined an involuntary sorority with Mary and Martha. There are gallons and gallons of tears spilling forth from the pages of God's Word, but within every story, we see God faithfully intervening and bringing hope and healing to those He loves so very deeply. There is no problem you could ever have that the Bible isn't interested in. There are no answers that are not written within its pages. You can glean so many nuggets of truth from these precious, sacred words to heal the hurt and give encouragement which the world simply cannot give. Such is the purpose of this book.

I have an assignment for you before you dive into the rest of this book. You didn't know you'd have homework before you even finished the first chapter! First, find a match and a candle. Take them with you to your favorite room in your home, and get comfortable there. Now make the room as dark as you can. Cut off all the lights, pull the curtains and unplug the nightlights. Make sure no light seeps in under the door. When darkness has fallen over the entire room, light your candle.

Even though I'm not sitting there with you, I know that an amazing thing just happened. The truth of Scripture was just proven! Skeptics must pack up and go home because you've just shown with this simple act that Scripture is true and God is who He says He is! Did you miss that? As you sit with this book in one hand and a candle in the other, allow me to explain!

John 1:5 says, *"The Light shines in the darkness, and the darkness did not comprehend it."* When you lit the candle, the fire gave off light. The light shined in the room and in that space, and in that moment, darkness was pushed back and your part of the world was illuminated. Things that you could not see when you sat in total darkness are now made clear. The light of the candle shows you what you need to see. If you should decide to walk around your darkened room, the candle will give you enough light to take the next step. It won't show you what the rest of your house looks like, and it certainly won't cast light on the sidewalk a mile away. But that's okay. It serves as a lamp unto your feet by giving you enough light to take the next step.

Grief can be a very dark time in your life. It's hard to know what to do in the dark. You need light to shine in your surroundings to know where to turn. Jesus said *"I am the Light of the world; he who follows Me will not walk in the darkness, but will have the Light of life."* (John 8:12). He has promised to be with you through all of life's joys and sorrows. He's with you on your journey through miscarriage.

If you could have a face-to-face conversation with Jesus Christ today, what would you say to Him? What would you ask Him? What do you imagine Him saying to you? Envision Jesus Christ Himself peering outside of the pages of Scripture and speaking straight into the baby-shaped void in your heart. What do you need Him to say to your broken heart? Friend, hear Him speaking to you through the Biblical stories of people just like yourself.

Let's examine some of these true stories of Scripture together. Let's join David on the battlefield. Perhaps you'll pick up some armor and weapons to help you fight your war. Kneel down beside Mary as she pours her oil on the feet of her Master. Smell the fragrance of true sacrifice. Eavesdrop on the disciples at Calvary. You'll find understanding from a Father who has Himself grieved the death of His Baby, and perhaps your heart will begin to heal.

Now, blow out your candle and turn the light back on. We have quite a journey ahead of us!

The Dance of Love & Sorrow

⸎

The music begins soft and sweet. The strains of a precious melody fill the air. Not the heavy, pressing beat of a march or the loud, thunderous sound of brass and percussion, but the sweet, gentle tune of a lullaby. You have stood on the edge of the dance floor through so many repetitions, but now your name has finally been called. Taking your partner's hand in yours, you step out on the dance floor and begin to fall into rhythm. Swaying this way and that with grace and ease, you relax in the wondrous joy of the moment as you ponder what your new life as a parent will be. Smiles. Coos. Rocking a sleeping baby snuggled securely against your chest in the stillness of the early morning hours. What joyous moments await you!

Without warning, the music changes. Instead of the soft and sweet strains of a lullaby, suddenly you hear the aching, sad sound of a funeral dirge. This long anticipated waltz through pregnancy now becomes a gut-wrenching tangle between life and death. You cannot believe that what started out as the most beautiful music you had ever heard is now a horrible, terrifying ballet. Hope and dread join hands and encircle you. The delicate struggle of life versus death takes over the dance floor and in a moment almost inconceivable you realize that, at least for the moment, death has won.

Death is so cruel. It laughs and taunts you as it twirls around the dance floor. "May I have this dance?" "No!" you cry with every ounce of strength within you. Death ignores your answer and takes its place within the dance floor of your womb. Not every duo is

17

interrupted. Some are even unaware of Death's presence. This baby spared. That baby saved. Your baby stolen. At one time, the news of a pregnancy took your breath away. Now you cannot breathe anyway. Not in the company of a foe as mighty as Death.

You are forced to leave the dance floor you have begged to join. "No! I cannot leave! It's too early! My dance is not complete!" But leave you must. You are led to the side of the dance floor once again, only to watch other couples twirl and spin, apparently hearing a tune you heard only for a moment. You stand there dumbfounded. You don't know what to do. You can't make sense of anything. You can't see. You can't hear. You can't breathe. You can't feel. You can't do anything to join this dance again. "Oh, there will be other dances, other songs." But this comfort is meaningless. You love *this song*. Sure, you could love another, but the melody and strains of *this song* captured your heart and your step. Why did *this dance* have to be destroyed?

You have never realized that numbness really is a precious gift, but now the numbness gives way to pain that you never could have previously imagined. When your name was called to join the dance, your heart was so full you thought it would literally burst inside you. Now, you believe it has. Fear and despair wrap their arms tightly around a heart now so empty that it simply cannot stand the pressure. It's beginning to crumble inside. It's much like your womb and your nursery. Empty. Empty. Empty.

For others, the dance continues. Some dances are different. Some have unique choruses, different composers. But for you, the music dies. The joy dies. All because your baby died. You cry out to loved ones, "Come near to me! Help me!" At the same time you scream, "Go away!" Nothing matters. Nothing makes sense. You learned the dance steps. You moved in time to the music. You did what everyone else did. Yet they receive a precious treasure, and you receive a death notice.

In this moment, you stand face to face with the most terrifying nightmare you have ever experienced and you wonder if anyone cares. Even with the passage of time, the memory of the music brings pain instead of pleasure. You can't even function in the most mundane of daily tasks, for all that remains in your heart and mind are the memories of the dance. The dance that ended when love and sorrow embraced.

But one day, you begin to hear music again. Very faint, but oh, so sweet. What is that sound? You strain to hear, but it remains far off. After a time you notice that the song is getting stronger, louder. And in one precious moment, you find yourself beginning to hum along. What is this song? Healing and hope join together to sing the most beautiful aria that has ever been written. A song of hope. A song of peace. A song of the promise of an eternal reunion with the child you held in your heart much longer than in your body. Somehow, you realize that you are beginning to sing again.

Where is the song coming from, and who is singing it? Who is this Master Musician? How does He know just what to sing? He's a Father who has Himself experienced the crushing death of His Child. A Child He has loved with a divine love. But wait! There are chords in this song you have never heard before! Beautiful chords. Comforting sounds. The Composer has written into this tune understanding. Patience. Healing. All intertwined with the anticipation of Heaven. Who is this Composer? This Father who was willing to orchestrate the death of His own Child, to offer you an eternal reunion with yours? He's *your* Father. And He stands ready to sing with you. To teach you new songs. Songs of hope, songs of joy. Songs that, although muted for a while, did not end when your dance ended.

You will survive this great sorrow.

You will live again. You will laugh again. You will sing again.

And whatever the song He has chosen for you,
you will dance again.

A Tsunami of Grief

In December of 2004, every news broadcast on every network had the same focus. Reporters were not interested in the national deficit or the rising cost of gasoline. Countries ravaged by war took a secondary place in the lineup. The only thing that people read about in the newspapers or on the internet, and the only discussion around the water coolers was the massive tsunami that devastated Southeast Asia. The death toll has been estimated to be as high as 289,000 men, women and children, though the exact number may never be known.

Grief is the tsunami of your heart. Much like those in Southeast Asia, you may have been totally unaware of looming disaster. You may have seen the warning signs, but knew that you were powerless to hold back the waters. Whatever the case may be, now that your baby has died, your heart, much like the shores of Sri Lanka, is being pounded by wave after wave of unbelievable, indescribable grief. You may think for a moment that the grief has subsided. You can begin to heal. But with the news of a friend's problem-free pregnancy, or the story of yet another baby forced to die at the hands of an abortionist, the tidal wave of sorrow finds its way to your heart and mind again. Your heart just keeps churning in the waters of sorrow and you can find no steady ground. All you see is death and destruction. All you know is sorrow beyond words. All you desire is for life to return to some semblance of normalcy.

In the midst of your fear and tumult, lift your head for a moment and look out into the storm. You just may see Someone calmly strolling through the crashing waves. Remember that even when the storms of life are battering you fiercely, there is One who comes to you, and He comes speaking a precious message: *Peace*. Just one word from the Master, and winds and waves have no choice but to be still. This is the same Lord who loved you enough to die for you. Why would you think that He would leave you to fend for yourself in the midst of a raging storm?

A Sleepy Savior

*35On that day, when evening came, He said to them,
"Let us go over to the other side." 36Leaving the crowd, they took
Him along with them in the boat, just as He was; and other boats
were with Him. 37And there arose a fierce gale of wind, and the
waves were breaking over the boat so much that
the boat was already filling up.
38Jesus Himself was in the stern, asleep on the cushion;
and they woke Him and said to Him, "Teacher, do You
not care that we are perishing?"
39And He got up and rebuked the wind and said to the sea,
"Hush, be still." And the wind died down and
it became perfectly calm.
Mark 4:35-39*

*25And He said to them, "Where is your faith?" They were fearful
and amazed, saying to one another, "Who then is this, that He
commands even the winds and the water, and they obey Him?"
Luke 8:25*

Have you ever experienced turbulence on an airplane? I'm not talking about a little bounce here and there. I'm talking about the kind of rocking and rolling that has nothing to do with music, but the kind that makes you wish you had never watched all those disaster movies about downed aircraft! Want to know what comforts me most on a bumpy ride? Not the exit rows. Not the belief that a tiny two-inch strap of canvas could keep me safe if I go hurtling through the sky. It's not even the fact that there's a barf bag waiting to catch my cookies should I be forced to toss them. The most comforting thing to me on a turbulent flight is a bored, sleepy flight attendant.

Bored to tears. Yawning. Stretching. Catching her balance enough to glance at her watch. Why does this make me feel better? Because she's been on rough rides before and she's not the least bit worried. When I start to get nervous, all I have to do is to look at her and her expression lets me know that everything is okay. She knows the pilot is in control even if the ride is bumpy. Together they have carried so many gazillions of passengers before me and there are gazillions more to come. The flight attendant knows that the pilot knows what he's doing.

It's because of her faith in the pilot that I know I can trust him. I've been on many tumultuous plane rides, but I have never once stormed the cockpit to ask the pilot what he was going to do to ensure my safety. I didn't question his ability or rail on his lack of concern. I never even considered the thought that he'd forgotten that there was a passenger in seat 10C. Why? I knew that he knew what he was doing, even if I did not. My lack of understanding of air currents or engine thrust didn't diminish his ability to deliver me safe and sound to my destination. Even if he had explained to me how the engines worked and how this massive, mechanical bird could lift off the ground and sail away to nearly any destination on this globe, I wouldn't understand it anyway. I didn't have to. I just sat down, strapped myself in for the ride and trusted that my pilot knew where to take me and how to get me there. Then I asked a very bored, very sleepy flight attendant for a Coke!

Do you realize that Jesus is simply not worried about your life? It's not that He's unconcerned, He's just not worried. He doesn't sit around and wring His holy hands wondering how He's going to pull you through the trauma of miscarriage. He's like the flight attendant who never blinks an eye when the plane bounces from cloud to cloud. When you find yourself getting scared because you feel so out of control since your baby died and you're beginning to doubt that you will reach your ultimate destination, glance at Jesus.

See the calm that He brings. No panicked look on His face! He knows the Pilot, and He knows that together you're going to arrive safely at your destination. In fact, you may even find Him napping in your ship!

Jesus was the ultimate teacher! We read that He and His disciples spent all day in an outdoor classroom of thousands while Jesus taught people with parables, using every day occurrences to teach them eternal truths. There were so many hungry for His message that Jesus had to literally stand in a boat to teach the people pressing in to get closer to Him. As night fell and Jesus had shared all He needed to share that day, they picked up their oars, turned Jesus' teaching podium into His chosen mode of transportation, and headed for the country of the Gerasenes. Everyone had to be exhausted! Let's eavesdrop a little on this worn-out band of followers as they set sail on one of the most life-changing nights of their lives.

As they settled down into their respective places on the boat, the conversation must have centered on the day's highlights. "Did you see the farmer with the pouch of seeds on his side? He almost swallowed his tongue when Jesus reached out and used his future crop to teach a lesson about sowing on good soil!" Jesus teaching, thousands learning, lives being forevermore changed. Learning at the knee of the Creator of the Universe must have made it such an exciting time to be alive! At some point during this animated discussion, Jesus slipped away to the stern of the boat, snuggled down into a cushion and drifted off to sleep.

How do you visualize Jesus? What do you think you would have seen with your physical eyes if you had had the privilege of seeing Him in the flesh? Tanned, leathery skin of a hard-working carpenter? Shoulders bent in grief when Lazarus died? Fire dancing in His eyes when He spoke of His Father? Muscular arms wrapping around His mother when she was cold? However you envision Him, as you ponder this incident in His earthly assignment, I want you to picture Him yawning! That's right! A sleepy Savior! When Jesus wrapped Himself in frail humanity, He took on all that is common to man, and that included fatigue!

As you travel through your journey of grief, you'll discover emotional lows you never dreamed existed. You'll also find that grief takes a toll on your physical body. You may find that you tire easily or are even more prone to illness. Jesus was tired so He slept. Just as Jesus did that day, learn how to take care of yourself physically and emotionally after your miscarriage.

Take care not to compare yourself to others who may be "hurting worse" than you. *"At least I have one child…" "She's had five miscarriages, I've only had one…," "I lost my baby so early, but theirs was full term…"* Stop. Just because someone else is hurting too, or may have more losses than you, doesn't mean you're not hurting.

Let's pretend that you and I were in a car accident together. (Okay. I know what you're thinking! This book was supposed to encourage me! What's this all about? Hang on a minute and you'll get my point!) In this accident, which for the sake of the story was not my fault or yours, I suffered a broken arm and you suffered a broken leg. 911 is quickly contacted and help soon arrives. As we are sitting on stretchers with paramedics at our sides, I hear you say, "No, I'm not going to go to the hospital. My leg is broken, but my arm is fine. I don't have a broken arm like my friend. My injury is not as important as hers." You may think this is a misprint, or that this manuscript was just not edited very well. Neither is true. Go back to the scene of the accident. "I'm not going to have treatment done to my injury. My friend has a broken arm and she has to get it set! Don't worry about the fracture in my femur. Go put a cast on my friend's arm!"

This would be absurd, wouldn't it? If we were unfortunate enough to be in an automobile accident and we were both injured, we would both need to allow medical personnel to treat our wounds. Why not let supportive friends and family do the same for you? We often find ourselves not wanting to take away from someone we feel has suffered a greater loss. My broken arm is a different hurt than your broken leg. Some of the experience is similar. Some is different. Just because I'm hurting, doesn't mean that you are not.

Would you walk around on your broken leg? If your leg is broken and you don't do what needs to be done to allow healing to take place, you will most likely walk with a painful limp for the rest of your life. No one wants to go to the hospital and be immobilized with a cast for several weeks, but that's what needs to happen for the bone in your leg to heal. No one wants to talk out his or her grief and hurt. No one wants to face life without their baby. Some don't want to commune with a God who didn't spare their child. But these are the things that must happen for healing to occur. Too bad we can't put a cast on your heart.

Before long, the disciples must have noticed the wind picking up. Remember that these guys were outdoorsmen and they knew weather patterns. They knew they were about to get sloshed as waves started splashing over the rails! The lessons learned in the daylight soon vanished in the darkness of night as they were frantically flinging handfuls of water back into the sea. Wind whipped around them as water filled their vessel. How would they ever survive a storm so great?

But wait a minute! Where was Jesus? The waves that terrified the disciples literally rocked the Master to sleep! The howling of the storm became His lullaby and the Creator of Heaven and earth rested His holy head on a pillow and went to sleep! Jesus never did anything half-way, so why would you think He only dozed? Maybe He snored and maybe He even slobbered, but I believe Jesus was out like a light! Do you think He dreamed? Perhaps He dreamt of going back to His Father's house. Maybe His eyes danced beneath slumbering eyelids as He dreamt of the day He'd reunite you and your baby there. Whatever the case was, He simply didn't worry about the storm.

Can you imagine what the disciples must have thought? One by one, each man started doing all he could do to ensure their survival. Peter pitching water back into the pitching waves, Matthew tying down a sail, John securing a rope, James tumbling as he tossed an anchor overboard! No doubt the disciples were doing everything they knew to do to get through the storm, and they probably assumed Jesus was being a good sailor as well.

At some point, somebody realized that Jesus wasn't helping. Maybe above the roar of the winds and the crashing of the waves someone heard Jesus snore! They simply couldn't believe what they were seeing! Jesus was asleep! I wonder if someone thought He was hurt since He was lying on the floor. That probably would have been easier to accept than the realization that He was simply snoozing.

Why wasn't He doing anything to assist? He worked a physically taxing job as a carpenter and He walked everywhere He went. He had to be in great shape physically. Why wouldn't He lift even one holy finger to help them in their storm?

As they shook their heads trying to gain focus and wiped the water out of their eyes, someone must have stomped over to Jesus, woke Him up and said "Don't you care if we perish out here? Save us, Jesus! We're about to drown! *Why don't you care?*"

Are you beginning to feel a connection with these rain-soaked sailors? Crying out to a silent sky, begging God to spare the life of your much-desired baby is a terrifying experience. As you stand drenched in the storm of sorrow, grab the side of the boat and hang on. The Master of the Sea just woke up!

I think it's very interesting that we don't know who actually woke Jesus up. All three accounts of this story in Scripture say "*they* came to Him..." or "*they* woke Him..." Hey, I don't blame them! Would you want your name to go down in history as the one who woke up Jesus and told Him that you didn't think He cared enough to save you? I wonder what "they" thought when they stood at Calvary?

Without argument and without delay, Jesus simply got up, looked out over the howling storm, rebuked the winds and said to the sea: "*Peace, be still.*" (Mark 4:39 KJV) I would love to have been there! Okay, I wouldn't necessarily want to be thrown from one end of the craft to the other as the storm raged, but I would love to have been there when the storm abruptly ceased! Can you picture it? The waves that were throwing their boat up in the air like a cat tossing a toy are suddenly as quiet and still as glass! The wind that cut through them like a knife is no more. They push their hair out of their eyes and with mouths hanging open take in the expression on Jesus' face. The howling of the wind has given way to the sound of men gasping in astonishment as they realize the storm is gone. Jesus looks at them and simply asks them, "Where is your faith?" Rain-soaked friend, I ask you the same. *Where is your faith?*

Is your faith in the hands of the doctors? In spite of training and technology, there are times when medicine fails. Is your faith in money? Money tends to run out, you know. Is your faith in the relationships you've forged with others? Precious though they are, some relationships are strained to the breaking point as they weather the storm of infant loss. If your faith is anywhere else besides in the Son of God, your faith will fail you. Even if you have placed your faith in your "religion" it may fall. People are fallible. God and His Word are not. God is trustworthy and He will never abuse your faith or fall short of what He has promised.

The disciples' faith was apparently not fully placed in Jesus. However, I want you to notice something. When Jesus asked the men where their faith was and why they doubted, I don't believe He was angry or disappointed in them. Notice that Scripture tells us that He "rebuked" the wind, but He *spoke* to the disciples. It's no coincidence that Jesus used weather to change the lives of these first century weathermen. Remember that Jesus was—and is—the most magnificent teacher ever, and He used what the people under-stood most to teach them about what they understood the least. He used storms to teach about peace. He used the storm that threatened the disciples' very existence to teach them that He was in full and loving control of the winds and waves. He used His death to teach about life eternal. He can use a situation in which you believe He is absent to show you just how close He really is to you. Rather than your miscarriage being the tool that Satan uses to prove to you that you've been forgotten by Heaven, it can be the classroom in which the Son of God teaches you how much He loves you.

Has your faith died since the moment your baby died? Have you found your faith decreasing along with your hormone levels? If this is the hurt of your heart, listen as Jesus says to your storm, "Peace, be still." He doesn't rebuke you for your doubt. He rebukes the doubt. The same word and the same *Word* that calmed the storm for the disciples that night can calm your storm and bring you peace.

You may feel that you have not only lost your baby, but you've lost control. You tried everything you could to ensure a safe devel-opment for your baby, but something went horribly wrong. You couldn't control how the embryo divided. You couldn't control the tiny heartbeat. No matter how hard you tried, you couldn't control your blood pressure or your hormone levels. Now, you struggle to control emotions bouncing around your chest like a million ping-pong balls. You just can't seem to regain control of anything. Your storm is out of control.

Good news, friend. The storm isn't really out of control. It's just that it's not under *your* control. Look at the flabbergasted reply of Jesus' shipmates that day: "*Who then is this, that He commands even the winds and the water, and they obey Him?*" (Luke 8:25). These guys were no neophytes. They had already witnessed so much of what Jesus could do, but when He slapped the waves down with only a word from the Word, He stopped them dead in their doubting tracks! *Who is this Jesus?* This Jesus is the Prince of Peace who calms your angry tempest with only His voice. He's the same Jesus who knows you'll survive this storm whether you know you will or not. He's the same Jesus who brings His peace to you. Peace that passes all under-standing and simply doesn't make sense considering the situation you find yourself in is yours for the taking. Never worry that He'll run out of patience with you. Because of the Lord's mercies that are new every morning, we are not consumed. (Lamentations 3:22-23 KJV) Are you afraid that even the Prince of Peace is not enough to speak peace to your hurt? Worry no more. His grace is sufficient and His strength is perfected in your weakness (2 Corinthians 12:9). This is the Jesus who calms your storm.

There are three accounts of this story in Scripture. They all tell the same basic story with each writer adding specific, unique details. Go back and re-read each account. You'll notice something inter-esting. Reading from the New American Standard Bible, you'll find that Jesus was called by three different names: Master, Lord and Savior. Why does this matter? Let this little nugget of truth remind you that Jesus will be whatever you need Him to be as you heal from your loss.

Remember the sleepy flight attendant? Chances are, she knew before I ever kissed my husband goodbye and boarded the plane that we'd have less than smooth sailing that day. Pilots know the forecast before they ever head down the runway and they are prepared. My flight attendant was not caught off guard by the turbulence and she was prepared.

Isaiah 43:2 says, "*When you pass through the water, I will be with you; and through the rivers, they will not overflow you. When you walk through the fire, you will not be scorched, nor will the flame burn you.*" This is such a comforting truth! Is it comforting to know that you're going to pass through fire and water? Not necessarily. But there is great comfort in knowing that my heartache never caught God by surprise. Notice that the verse says *when* you pass through the water and the rivers. *When* you walk through the fire. Not *if,* but *when.* God knew long before you kissed your spouse goodbye and headed into the doctor's office that day that your life would drastically change. When you stood dumbfounded at the insensitivity of others who said such hurtful things, God was already there, knowing this difficulty would come. Deuteronomy 1:30 tells you that the Lord your God goes before you and He Himself will fight on your behalf. He knows *when* the heartache will come—not *if* it will come—and He goes before you to fight for you.

But don't stop there! Keep reading! When you pass through the waters God Himself will be with you so the rivers cannot overflow you! When you walk through the fire, you will not be scorched or burned! He knows when hurt is coming and He's ready! Ready to steady you when you think you'll fall from the weight of grief. Ready to speak peace to your heart when the waves are crashing around you. Ready to bring a calm as great as your storm.

Look at the final words of Mark 4:39: *and it became* **perfectly** *calm.* No matter how the winds raged and fear wrapped around the hearts of the sailors that day, when Jesus calmed their storm it became *perfectly* calm. He knows how to speak perfect calm into your life. Maybe that means that you will eventually bring home a healthy, full-term baby. Maybe your perfect calm involves living a wonderful and fulfilling life without children, or with fewer children than you wanted to have. As impossible as these scenarios seem, realize that God is a magnificent Creator and He knows just how to speak an impossible peace into the storm of your life. Confused as to how a life without children could possibly be the perfect calm to follow your storm? Don't worry about it. The disciples never dreamed the answer to their storm rested in a sleeping Savior! Proverbs 4:5-6 releases you from the burden of having to understand all that God does. Lean not on your own understanding. You don't have to understand what God is doing. In fact, He lovingly tells you not to! Just trust Him. He'll take care of the storm.

After the storm passed, Jesus and this unlikely crew sailed through calm, still waters to a place called the Gerasenes. As the disciples tried to force the water out of their still soggy ears, Jesus was focused on the divine appointment that awaited Him, and I believe Satan was fighting Him every inch of the way. What was so important that Jesus would brave a life-threatening storm? Someone needed Him.

Who was this "someone"? It must have been someone important, right? Someone who could help Him further His ministry? Someone who would contribute financially to His work? No, not this someone. This someone was naked, and running through the tombs screaming to the top of his lungs. This someone was so far out of his mind that he didn't even know his own family. This someone was possessed with so many demons that you'd think Someone as holy as the Son of God wouldn't want anything to do with him. But this someone needed Jesus, so not even the wildest storm or the strongest wind could keep Him from the shores of the Gerasenes.

Jesus cleansed and healed this pitiful monument to the fall of humanity when He cast the demons out of the man that day. He was later found at the feet of Jesus, clothed and in his right mind, memorizing every word his newfound Savior had to say. Can you imagine the unbelievable relief his family must have felt when Jesus sent him home? Their anguish gave way to mind-boggling celebration!

You see, Satan didn't want Jesus to get to the Gerasenes because he knew a great miracle was waiting on the shores. Perhaps it's the same for you. Satan doesn't want you to survive this grief because he knows there is a great miracle waiting for you. Can you imagine what God wants to do in your life as a result of the great trial you are surviving?

Maybe you feel like you're not strong enough to survive this storm. You feel too fragile to survive the strong winds that toss you to and fro, and you fear becoming a statistic of the storm. Unless you moved to Mars for a while, you are undoubtedly aware of the devastation my south Louisiana homeland faced during the late summer of 2005 when Louisiana and other parts of the Gulf Coast were ravaged by the devastating Hurricane twins, Katrina and Rita. Waves pounded our shorelines and floodwaters rose, commanding destruction on everything in their paths. Lifetimes of memories were washed away as people stared with numbed hearts as everything they'd ever worked for washed down the streets in a torrent of mud and sludge. It was really quite surreal. For weeks, you'd drive down the streets and see people walking aimlessly and they all had the same look on their faces. It was as if their expressions were trying to convey what their words simply could not: "What do we do now?"

I remember during Hurricane Katrina, I looked out the window in my front door to see if I could tell if our neighborhood was still there. What I saw amazed me! I didn't see the tree down the street whose roots had lifted from 30 feet below ground. I didn't even notice the side of the house missing across the street from my own. What got my attention that day as rain pelted the windows and winds blew with such force? A butterfly. A beautiful yellow butterfly was trying her best to weather Hurricane Katrina's might that day. I only saw her for a moment and she was gone. But in that moment, I saw you.

Though the winds were howling, this butterfly was trying with all her might to survive. She was flittering as best she could, taking her place in the air as the debris was flying. She never gave up, though I'm sure her butterfly friends may have told her that it was simply impossible to survive. But she kept going. I'll never forget the sight of a butterfly in a hurricane! It was beautiful. It was as if God planted a reminder in the middle of a hurricane that new life was coming after the storm.

A struggle? Sure. But remember, that butterfly has struggled before. The struggle to emerge from a caterpillar's cocoon to take its place in the Master Gardener's grand scheme of life as a beautiful butterfly. Was life the same? No. It never will be again. The butterfly doesn't crawl around as the caterpillar did. She soars! She had to fight to get out of the cocoon or she surely would have died there. But God had greater plans. He wanted her to soar from flower to flower. He wanted her to dance on the breeze of a warm summer day. And He wanted to bring her through the fury of a hurricane.

Who knows what God has planned for your life as you struggle to survive your miscarriage? Life won't be the same as you dreamed it would be. But just as we learn from the life of David, your life doesn't have to end because your baby's did. Study the storms we see in Scripture. Jesus was right there in the middle of them, never leaving his beloved for a moment. On the surface, God does things that just don't make sense, but if you hold on you'll see that He truly has a magnificent plan for your life and He really is working all things for your good. God knows just how to bring you forth from the cocoon of sorrow and grief and watch you emerge victorious! He can bring you through the fury of a hurricane even if you feel as weak and timid as a tiny butterfly. All it takes is the voice of the Master of the sea saying, "Peace, be still." Even hurricane force winds are powerless to defeat a tiny butterfly if God says she'll make it through the storm. You, my friend, will make it too.

Strolling Through Sorrow

∽∾

Even Jesus' closest earthly friends feared storms. They knew too much about them to take them lightly. Several of them were fishermen, and Jesus called them to service as they worked their jobs on the seashore. When the winds began to howl and the water splashed over the sides of the boat, Jesus' disciples got more than a little nervous. The Sea of Galilee was known for its huge, unpredictable and unexpected storms. They rose with little or no warning and could have toppled any craft trying to cross. The storms rose. The disciples panicked. The waves crashed. James and Andrew started tying things down. Jesus went for a stroll and invited Peter to come along!

Perhaps that's what He says to you today. *"Come along. Don't weather the storm of grief alone. Come with Me. Walk with Me."* And just as He did when His friends faced their own storms, He'll say to your storm *"Peace, be still."*

Join me on a journey, won't you? Bring your broken heart and let's climb up in the boat with Jesus' disciples. Let's see what Jesus says to us when the dark clouds gather. But friend, don't forget to grab your umbrella and put on your raincoat. We're headed for a quite a storm!

****

²²Immediately He made the disciples get into the boat and go ahead of Him to the other side, while He sent the crowds away. ²³After He had sent the crowds away, He went up on the mountain by Himself to pray; and when it was evening, He was there alone. ²⁴But the boat was already a long distance from the land, battered by the waves; for the wind was contrary. ²⁵And in the fourth watch of the night He came to them, walking on the sea. ²⁶When the disciples saw Him walking on the sea, they were terrified, and said, "It is a ghost!" And they cried out in fear. ²⁷But immediately Jesus spoke to them, saying, "Take courage, it is I; do not be afraid."

²⁸Peter said to Him, "Lord, if it is You, command me to come to You on the water."

²⁹And He said, "Come!"

And Peter got out of the boat, and walked on the water and came toward Jesus. ³⁰But seeing the wind, he became frightened, and beginning to sink, he cried out, "Lord, save me!" ³¹Immediately Jesus stretched out His hand and took hold of him, and said to him, You of little faith, why did you doubt?"
³²When they got into the boat, the wind stopped.
³³And those who were in the boat worshiped Him, saying, "You are certainly God's Son!"
Matthew 14:22-33

⁵¹Then He got into the boat with them, and the wind stopped; and they were utterly astonished, ⁵²for they had not gained any insight from the incident of the loaves, but their heart was hardened.
Mark 6:51-52

²¹So they were willing to receive Him into the boat, and immediately the boat was at the land to which they were going. ²²The next day the crowd that stood on the other side of the sea saw that there was no other small boat there, except one, and that Jesus had not

entered with His disciples into the boat,
but that His disciples had gone away alone.
John 6:21-22

I love the story of Peter walking on the water with Jesus. It is one I have heard my entire life, and no doubt, if you've ever been to Sunday school in your life, you've heard it too. Jesus walking on the water, Peter walking with Him, Peter sinking, Jesus pulling Him back up again. End of story—move on to the next chapter, right?

Slow down! There's so much in this story we can learn from! One thing I love about the Bible is how incredibly relevant it is to every situation in our everyday lives. We can even find truths in this storm to help you weather the storm of your miscarriage or the tempest of the stillbirth of your baby! But what does Peter walking on the water have to do with the fact that your baby died? I am so glad you asked!

The disciples of Jesus were men who were blessed to see the Son of God in the flesh. They saw the expressions on His face, heard the tone of His voice, felt the touch of His hand on their shoulders. Their lives became a classroom where they lived every day learning from the Creator of all. Sometimes God's lesson plans included storms.

In the Bible, there are several accounts of the day that Jesus fed 5,000 men, their wives and their children with only five small loaves of barley and two tiny sardines. Imagine Philip as he realized that the rumble he heard coming from that Galilean hillside wasn't the sound of wild animals coming to attack them, but was in reality the growling of at least 15-20,000 empty stomachs! "Jesus! What are we gonna do? It would take at least eight months wages to feed all these people!" That's when unassuming Andrew somehow knew that Jesus could provide, and brought to Him the original "Happy Meal". A tiny portion fed a huge multitude. You'd think that as the disciples rubbed their full bellies, they'd really believe Jesus could really do anything. Wouldn't you?

Following this impromptu "dinner on the grounds", Jesus told the people to go home, and told the disciples to go on to the boat and head out for the other side of the Lake. They did as Jesus told them to do. Jesus' buddies left Him on the shore and headed out for the other side of the Lake. No doubt, their thoughts were as deep as the water they sailed through as they contemplated the miracle they had just seen.

All of a sudden, the silence of their evening cruise was broken. The wind started to pick up, and their boat began to pitch back and forth. Whew! Those barley loaves were feeling a little heavy in their stomachs now! Lightning flashed! Thunder roared! Like the tempest around them, fear drenched the men as they began to realize that Jesus was not with them in this storm.

Why did Jesus abandon them? Was He afraid of the storm? Did it catch Him off guard? If He really knows the future, why did He go traipsing off to the mountains rather than get on board the ship to help steer the way to the other side of this problem?

Sound familiar? "God, why did You abandon me when I needed You most? Are you as afraid as I am? Do You really know everything? Then why didn't You help my doctor find the problem in time? Jesus, did the death of my baby catch You off guard? If You are really in control, why didn't You stop my early labor? God, where were You in my storm?"

Maybe anger is the storm that surrounds your life. Your fury churns like deep waters when you wonder where God was when your baby lost the battle for life. Friend, if this is the cry of your wounded heart, don't abandon ship just yet. The answer is coming—walking straight to you on the waters of your hurt.

Allow me to direct your attention to verse 23 of Matthew chapter 14. *"After He had sent the crowds away, He went up on the mountain by Himself to pray;"* (You'll also find this nugget of truth in John 6:15 and Mark 6:46.) Jesus had not abandoned them. Not even for a moment. Rather, He was doing the most important thing He could have done while His friends were having a problem. He was praying.

Do you realize that Jesus prays for you? He was praying for you long before you ever knew you'd have a problem with your pregnancy. Long before you drew your first breath, long before you realized that your baby never would, Jesus prayed for you. How do we know? Look at Hebrews 7:24-25: *"...but because Jesus lives forever, he has a permanent priesthood. Therefore he is able to save completely those who come to God through him, because he always lives to intercede for them."* (NIV) Jesus is interceding to God the Father for us! Jesus stands face to face with God and talks to Him about you! Can you imagine what He says? "Father, these are my children. The death of their baby has been so hard on them. But Your grace is sufficient for even so great a hurt as this. Send the comfort of the Holy Spirit to them." Jesus sits at the right hand of God—the power side of God—and speaks to God on your behalf (Romans 8:34)! When your hurt is too deep for words and you find that you cannot even pray for yourself, Romans 8:26 tells you that the Spirit Himself intercedes for you with groanings too deep for words. Jesus prays for you!

Meanwhile, the disciples are stuck in the middle of a fierce gale. The wind is howling, and Jesus is praying. The waves are washing over the side of their craft, and Jesus is praying. They are being tossed side to side and no doubt, they are beginning to fear for their lives, and Jesus is praying. Many a Galilean fisherman perished in storms like this, just as many marriages perish in the storms of infant death. If it feels like no one cares, that no one wants to look at the hurt in your heart, take heart. Jesus is praying. He's praying for you! As wonderful as this truth is, there's more! Jesus not only prays for you, but He *sees* your storm.

Jesus prayed up on a mountain and the disciples' boat was about 3 to 3 ½ miles out from shore (John 6:19). The disciples probably couldn't see Him because they had their eyes on the water splashing in their faces. They were so wrapped up in securing the boat to try to ride out the storm that they probably didn't take the time to look around for Jesus. They were probably convinced that He had no clue that the storm was threatening them so. Not only was Jesus aware of the problem, not only was Jesus praying for them, but Jesus actually saw what was going on! Jesus saw the waves rising up. Mark 6:48 says that Jesus saw the disciples straining at the oars. Jesus saw the looks on their faces. More importantly, Jesus saw the fear in their hearts and He knew just when to step in and calm the sea for them.

Jesus has not abandoned you in your storm. Jesus sees you when you don't know how to answer the one who asks how far along you are in your pregnancy now. Jesus sees when you cannot walk past the empty nursery down the hall. Jesus sees you when you see a pregnant woman or healthy newborn baby. He sees every tear that streams down your face, even those that flow today. Most importantly, He sees the hurt and fear in your heart, and just like He knew on the Sea of Galilee, He knows just when to step in and calm the sea for you.

Are you wondering where Jesus is? It's so easy to focus so intently on the broken pieces of your heart that you simply cannot see the face of Jesus. Tears cloud your vision like the waves that slapped the disciples' faces. Sorrow has gripped you so tightly and you are convinced that God has turned His head and cannot see the storm enveloping you. But look! Out there in the middle of the storm! Someone comes walking on the water. And He's headed straight for you.

Sometime between 3:00 and 6:00 A.M., the disciples are steadily battling the storm. With arms and backs aching from straining against the wind, calloused hands gripped ropes as tightly as the fear that gripped their hearts. Matthew 24:14 tells us that "the ship was tossed with waves: for the wind was contrary". The original meaning of the word tossed is actually "tortured". The disciples were being tortured by the storm they were fighting. The waves were coming in uninterrupted succession. Before the men had time to wipe the water from their faces, another surge would hit and the waves would crash over them again. They were literally being tortured as they tried their best to plow through unbelievable torrents of water. But the waves were not the only problem they faced that night. The wind was contrary. The literal meaning says the wind was their "adversary". They were being tortured by an uninterrupted succession of waves as they battled their adversary. Sound familiar? It should.

Death is never a welcomed guest in our families. Even when we have watched a loved one suffer in a body ravaged by disease and pain, if given the choice, we'd rather see them miraculously and instantaneously healed of any disease and watch them continue on in the realm of reality we share. We know that with the death of a Christian, Heaven awaits. We know that a life in Heaven means no sorrow, no disease, and no pain. We know death is an inevitable part of life for all of us. *What we don't know is how we'll ever survive the death of a baby.*

Maybe you feel like you should have been the first mate on the disciples' ship that day. Sorrow comes in like a flood. Before you can even regain your composure from the torture your adversary has thrown at you, another wave comes crashing in. Waves of sorrow. Waves of misunderstanding. Waves of anger. Waves of confusion. Who is this adversary? It's not your spouse. Your adversary is not insensitive friends and family members who tend to say the wrong things. It's not even the doctors and nurses who see your life-changing heartache as a medical issue that simply needs to be documented in a chart. No, friend. Your adversary is Satan himself.

Satan would love nothing more than for you to totally lose your relationship with God as a result of the storm you're weathering. He throws waves of misunderstanding in your path as he tells you that God is nowhere to be found in this storm. He taunts you and tells you that no one recognizes that you've lost a *baby*. It was only a few cells, anyway! Another wave of hurt. The whisper telling you that God surely doesn't love you as much as the woman to whom He has granted a houseful of healthy children that she doesn't even love? It brings about another wave of anger. You're being tortured by the adversary. Slip over, Peter. John, make room! Another sailor needs to find rest in your boat!

But never forget for a moment who your adversary *really* is! Satan, your adversary, is the father of lies. John 8:44 says, *"he (the devil) does not stand in the truth because there is no truth in him. Whenever he speaks a lie, he speaks from his own nature, for he is a liar and the **father of lies**."* When he tells you that God has forgotten you, and doesn't know the storm you're battling, remind him that Jesus said, *"Lo, I am with you always"* (Matthew 28:20) and that he is the father of lies. And when he tries to convince you that your baby was insignificant, that he or she didn't really matter, remind him that your baby, whether born or unborn, was created in the image and likeness of God, (Genesis 1:26) and that he, Satan, is the father of lies. Never forget who your adversary is! But never, ever forget who Jesus is!

Let's go back to our story! The disciples are desperately struggling to maintain control, fighting as hard as they know how to fight, and wondering if they really are going to survive this storm. However, in one life-changing instant, someone must have looked up from his oars and gazed out into the storm.

Verse 25 tells us very simply that Jesus came to the disciples, walking on the sea. Have you ever wondered why He decided to walk on the water? Couldn't He have just decided to be with them and instantaneously appeared on the ship? Why didn't He just solve their problem from the mountainside where He prayed? Did He have to be there in physical form to calm the sea? Of course not! So why did He walk on water to get to them? Remember that they were about 3-3.5 miles out. Why did He decide to take a stroll in the middle of this horrible storm?

I think the answer can be found in the original meaning of the word "walking". I love to find what the authors of these passages really held in their hearts as they held their pens in their hands. The true meaning of the message sometimes gets lost in translation, and the original definitions of the words can open up a whole new understanding for us. Such is the case with this passage of Scripture.

Jesus came to them, walking on the water. The original meaning of the word "walking" is "to walk at large, *especially as proof of ability*"! Jesus came to His disciples in the midst of one of the greatest storms of their lives to prove His ability to them! He could have looked down from the mountaintop and spoken the word and the seas would have instantly become as still as glass. But He had a greater plan. He could have prevented the storm from rising. But He had a greater plan. He could have allowed them to perish that day. But He had a greater plan. He wanted to prove to them in an undeniable fashion that He was able to calm any storm they encountered, and that He really knew how to speak peace to their hearts. And to yours.

Do you realize that Jesus came *walking*? He didn't come running. That would imply that He came later than He needed to. He came walking to them. He didn't come stumbling. He wasn't unsteady on His feet. He came walking to them. Scripture does not say that He was looking from side to side, or that He walked to the north and then to the east, and then changed His path and went west. He knew exactly what He was doing and where He was going. He came walking to them. He didn't come crawling. He would never bow down to this adversary! He came walking to them. And walking to them in a way that would showcase His ability!

Have you ever seen someone stroll into a room full of confidence, healthy, strong and with their mind totally on the task before them? Compare that person to the one who is sneaking in the room, trying to hide behind the nearest column or artificial tree, scared to death because they really have no business being there anyway. Or what about a person so sick they can hardly force one foot to land in front of the other without swaying from side to side? Jesus came walking to his friends with confidence in His own ability and ready to make a difference in their storm and in their lives. Without this storm in their lives, how could Jesus have proven to them His ability to calm a storm? What do you think would have made the more indelible impact on their lives—someone telling them the story of Jesus calming a storm, or the vision of Jesus walking confidently toward them while water splashed in their faces and the waves and their stomachs rolled? The storm simply laid the groundwork for Jesus to prove to them in an undeniable way that He really was who He said He was, and that He really could calm every storm they'd ever face.

Perhaps Jesus is saying the same thing to you today. He has been praying for you. He knows just when to step in. He knows how to calm your storm. This storm is not unseen by the Maker of Heaven and Earth. You have not been forgotten. Jesus comes walking on the water of your storm and He's coming *straight to you!* Look out through the waves. Don't let the fierceness of the lightning and thunder distract you from the One you see walking toward you on the waves. Just as the disciples did that night, peer through the raging tempest and see that Jesus is on the scene and on the water!

Picture the scenario. Who was it that first saw Jesus walking on the water? Was it Andrew? He was always bringing someone to Jesus. He would have loved to have brought this shipload of frightened, doomed men to the Savior that day! Was it Judas? I'll bet he would have tried to figure out how to make a buck off this super-natural feat! Sell the story to the Galilean Times!

Whoever it was, can you imagine the look of shock on his face when he saw the figure of a man walking on the water? We may not know who it was who first spotted Jesus, but we know they were all terrified. They thought He was a ghost! Picture it! One moment they're all straining against the oars just trying to survive, no doubt thinking that life couldn't get any worse than this, when all of a sudden, one of the men stops rowing. Just as his compatriots start to reprimand him for not pulling his weight, they notice the look on his face. He tries to stand although he's unsteady on his feet due to the tossing of the boat. With eyes wide and panicked, he drops the oar and points a trembling finger toward an unknown figure approaching their ship! "A ghost! AHHHHH!"

As if the chaos of the storm was not enough, now you have a boatload of petrified sailors battling storms on the inside and the outside. The physical storm that threatened their bodies was no match for the storm of fear threatening their hearts, and they were scared. Scared that they were not strong enough to conquer the storm. Scared that their families would never be the same. Scared of what would happen if they didn't survive. Scared of what would happen if they did.

Look in Matthew 14:26-27 and notice what Jesus did: [26] *"...And they cried out in fear. [27]But immediately Jesus spoke to them, saying, "Take courage, it is I; do not be afraid."* Jesus not only saw their storm and knew just when to step in, but He heard the cry of their hearts when they cried out in fear. There is a beautiful word in this verse that I want you to notice. The word is **"immediately"**. *Immediately* Jesus spoke to them telling them to take courage. *Immediately*, Jesus recognized their fear, and gave them reason to lay down their apprehension. *Immediately,* Jesus told them not to be afraid. He didn't wait for them to work their way through the storm. He didn't preach a whole new sermon to them before He met their need. No, friend. When the disciples' hearts were wrapped in the grip of fear, Jesus *immediately* spoke peace to their hearts and told them He was near.

Jesus stands near to you as you stand brokenhearted at your baby's gravesite. He walks through your storm to bring you a precious message: "Take courage! It is I! Don't be afraid!" Fear subsides when Jesus is near. You can have courage when Jesus is near. The storm isn't quite as scary when Jesus is near. James 4:8 says, "Draw nigh to God, and he will draw nigh to you." Just as the disciples cried out in fear that night on the crashing waves, cry out to God out of your fear. Draw nigh to Him. He'll draw near to you. He promises to never leave you, never forsake you. And when Jesus walks near on the stormy seas of your life, you'll find a way to have courage. You'll find a way to shed the fear. And maybe, just maybe, you'll find your way out of the boat!

I'd love to have seen the faces of the disciples when they realized that the apparition they thought they were seeing that night really was Jesus Himself. Mouths dropping open! Eyes wide! Confusion begging to give way to relief! What a night for these men. Jesus walking through the storm and on top of the water! Who would ever believe this? Surely, this was the most surreal thing He could do that night, right? Right? Wrong!

One of my favorite disciples would have to be Peter. I love this guy! Maybe he reminds me a little too much of myself! You know — speaking before he thinks things through. Getting angry a little too easily. Impetuous. Impulsive. Oh well! You just gotta love Peter!

Peter had been fighting the storm that night. He had been a fisherman, so chances are he had fought many a gale in his career. He had to know that the last thing you want to do in the middle of a storm is jump ship! He'd probably held on with white knuckles to the sides of many ships as they pitched back and forth on dangerously crashing waves. Doesn't it make sense that Peter would be the one to do something outrageous? That Peter would be the one to take a chance, and climb out of the boat?

Matthew 14:28 tells us that once Peter realized that it was Jesus strolling through the waves, that he cried out to Jesus saying, "Lord, if it is You, command me to come to You on the water." Can you imagine what his buddies must have thought? "Oh, Peter! For once, can't you just be like everybody else and help us fight this storm? Just help Jesus into the boat — don't climb out of it yourself!

45

What are you thinking, man?" Maybe they decided that Peter was going to do what Peter wanted to do, so they may as well save their breath. (I think it's interesting that of the three accounts of this story in Scripture, Matthew was the only one who included the part about Peter walking on the water. I guess with all of Peter's shenanigans, jumping out of a boat in the middle of a storm wasn't significant enough for them all to include it in their writings!) I don't think Peter heard a word they said, or even cared what they thought. All he focused on in that moment was Jesus' response to his request: "Come."

I picture Jesus and Peter with their eyes locked on each other with laser beam intensity, as Jesus simply said, "Come!" He didn't reprimand him for being afraid, although we know he was. Remember that verse 26 says, "*they* were terrified". It doesn't say, "All but Peter were scared, but Peter was so brave and confident that he sat whistling as he rowed." There is also no record of Jesus having to stop and think about His response. He just told Peter to come on out of that boat. He gave him no instructions. He didn't tell him what He had planned. One word from the Word and Peter's life would never be the same. *"Come."*

At Jesus' command, Peter climbed out of the boat and walked on the water to Jesus. How did Peter step out on the water? Hesitantly? Not Peter. I believe he thrust his foot out there just as he would have if he were stepping from the boat onto a pier or the beach. Maybe he jumped! Chances are he did not touch his toe to the water to see if it felt okay before deciding to put his weight down on the splashing waves. No, with his eyes still locked on Jesus', the water turned as solid as concrete beneath Peter's feet that day as he began his journey to Jesus!

Back up with me for a moment. Remember when we first see Jesus walking on the water towards the disciples? Remember the original meaning of the word "walking"—"as proof of ability"! Fasten your seat belts! This is the same word used to describe how Peter walked to Jesus that night! Peter stepping out the boat that night was proof of Jesus' ability! His ability to keep Peter safe in his storm! His ability to know that Peter had a problem, but Jesus had the answer! Peter's stepping out of the boat was simply a step of faith to prove the ability of the Master! What an honor for Peter! What a beautiful way to view Peter's storm!

Now that you have experienced the excruciating storm of the death of your baby, others are watching you. When your baby died, the storm rose and seemed that it would destroy you. But Jesus comes walking through your storm. You have been stripped of your ability. If you had had the ability to save your baby's life you would have done it without a moment's hesitation. You would have mortgaged your home, forsaken the land you love, embraced a lifetime of labor to save the life of this tiny, little soul. But your abilities were not enough. If you had the ability to remove the hurt from your spouse's eyes, you'd do it today. If you had the ability to speak peace to his or her heart and hurt, you'd have no need for this book or any other. But as mere mortals, we lack the ability to erase the hurt and sorrow that death brings. Jesus knows this. He knows that there was simply nothing else that you could do. However, Jesus Christ holds this ability in His hands and He knows just when to step in and calm the storm.

Can you imagine what Peter must have felt as he walked on the water toward Jesus? In that moment, his life was a living testament to the ability of the Christ! But his confidence apparently was short-lived. Go with me to the raging waters and let's see what happened next.

Verse 30 of Matthew 14 says that when Peter saw the winds howling about him, he became frightened again and started to sink. For one moment, he took his eyes off of Jesus and the storm began to overtake him. For one instant, he looked at the turmoil surrounding his life and didn't see Jesus standing calmly on top of the same waves that were threatening to destroy him. For one split second, Peter felt the fear and felt the concrete beneath him turn to water, and he began to sink.

As you journey through grief, you may really identify with Peter. You've found yourself in a massive storm, but you've been able to see Jesus walking toward you. At His command, you take a step of faith and climb out of the boat, trusting Him every step of the way. For a moment, the storm is not overtaking you. For a moment, the hurt seems to diminish, if only a little. For a moment, the embrace of love conquers the embrace of sorrow, the waters begin to recede and you begin to believe you're going to make it!

But then you hear a young mother call her living child by your dead child's name. The ground beneath you begins to give way. Perhaps everywhere you turn someone else is pregnant and having a perfectly routine pregnancy. A tidal wave of grief pummels you. A news reporter tells another story of an unwanted baby being ripped from the womb, when you would have given everything you own to keep your baby in yours. The winds are beginning to howl and you are beginning to sink. If so, you've just become a modern day Peter!

When Peter began to sink, he did the best thing he ever could have done. Peter cried out to Jesus. "Lord, save me!" Peter knew he could not save himself. More importantly, Peter knew that Jesus could! If you are finding yourself sinking again, do as Peter did. Cry out to Jesus. "Jesus, my heart is hurting so badly!" "Jesus! I don't know if I'm going to survive!" "Jesus! My marriage is falling apart!" "Jesus! Jesus! Jesus! Save me!"

Look what Jesus did when Peter cried out to Him. There's that wonderful word again! The very first word in verse 31 says it all: *Immediately*. Immediately Jesus stretched out His hand and took hold of him! Jesus didn't stand there with His hands on His hips and wait for Peter to confess every wrongdoing. He didn't wait for him to lay out a five-point plan as to how he would do differently next time. Jesus saw His child in trouble and immediately He stretched out His hand and pulled him to the surface once again. If you are sinking in dread or fear, cry out to Jesus. He didn't love Peter more than He loves you! He'll immediately grab hold of you. And here's the best part—He'll never let go!

As you keep reading through the end of this story, you will not find where Jesus let go of Peter's hand. He didn't pull him up out of the water, brush His hands off and push Peter into the boat. No! There is no record of Jesus letting go of his hand. Let this sink deep into your spirit. Jesus will not let go of your hand. He knows you cannot survive your miscarriage alone. He refuses to let go. Even if your faith has wavered like Peter's did. Even if the storm is raging at insane levels. Jesus refuses to let go.

Notice something else. When did Peter's storm cease? Do you realize that the storm did not cease when Peter stepped out of the boat? He had obeyed Jesus' command. He walked on the water to showcase Jesus' ability to be everything He promised He would be. You would think that would have been enough. He passed the test, right? But the storm kept raging. The wind kept blowing. The water kept splashing up on Peter's tunic. And Jesus kept walking on the water.

What about when Jesus pulled Peter back up out of the water after he sunk? Surely, the storm ceased then, right? Unh, uh. Read it for yourself. Even after he steadied Peter on his feet, there is no record of the wind dying down or the seas becoming calm yet. The answer is there in verse 32: When they got into the boat, the wind stopped.

So what does this mean to you? It means just as Jesus walked with Peter all throughout his storm, Jesus walks with you through yours. He may not calm your storm when you think He should, but the winds and the seas still have to bow down to His command. The fact that the storm kept going shows you that Jesus was never intimidated by the storm. He was still working and moving through Peter's storm—and yours.

Finally, go with me to one more verse. Verse 33: And those who were in the boat worshipped Him, saying, "You are certainly God's Son!" Others will see you as you battle. Some will watch with pity. Some will watch with understanding. Some will watch to see if God really will be what you've told them He will be. Maybe you've been the one wrapping your arms of comfort around hurting, grieving friends and reminded them that Jesus is the Prince of Peace. Maybe your spouse has been there for others, praying for the comfort of the Holy Spirit as they traveled through the storms of death, divorce or illness. But now, your ship is being tossed about by the adversary, and the winds are contrary against you. Now you are in the boat. Now they will watch to see how you survive the storm.

John 6:21 says that the disciples were willing to take Jesus into their boat. Are you willing to take Him into your boat? Are you willing to give Him your hurt, your fear, your anger? I'll bet your first reaction is something like this: "Are you kidding? Of course, I'll let Him take it from me! I want nothing more!"

Since the death of your baby, sorrow has defined who you are. If you let go of the hurt, what will you think about? Pray about? Talk about? Is it scarier to let go of the familiar—even if the familiar is excruciating—or to trust an unseen God with your future? A woman grieving the murder of her adult son said that she would never let go of her anger toward her child's murderer. The strength of the anger was the only strength she had. Without the anger, she felt she would collapse and die. Are you willing to allow Christ to take that from you?

You have an opportunity in your hurt and devastation to showcase God's ability to sustain you. What an opportunity! What an honor! Someone reading these words will think I'm insane for telling you that you can find an honor in this horrific sorrow. Some may weep. Some may close the book. But all will make a choice.

As you journey through grief, many choices are taken away from you. If you had the choice, you would have brought home a healthy, full-term baby. If you had the choice, you wouldn't need to read these stories. But there is one choice that you must make. The choice to trust God through the storm and showcase His ability, or to drown in the sorrow of grief and loss.

If you choose to trust God, you will receive blessings that you never could have experienced any other way. You'll see first hand how Jesus can calm a storm with nothing more than one word. You'll feel the strength of His hand as He pulls you up from the waters that could have drowned you. You'll bask in the sweet realization that He never for a moment let go of your hand. And you'll find that there really is a joy in allowing your life to be a display for the world to see the ability of God to sustain you through trials.

God, Surely You Blew It This Time!

꧂

What did you do when you first realized there was a problem with your pregnancy? What was your very first thought? "Oh, God! Help us!" Maybe your pregnancy was picture perfect. No morning sickness. No stretch marks. But no living baby in the delivery room. "God, where were you? God, why didn't you intervene? I know You've parted the waters! You've brought fire down from Heaven! You've turned water into wine! So why did you turn a deaf ear to my prayers to save the life of my baby? Oh God, surely You blew it this time!"

Most of us tend to pray when we're in trouble, even if we never pray any other time. Why do we do this? Do we really believe God *can* help? Do we really believe He *will*? We go to Him because we know that there are situations where man is helpless. No matter the magnitude of his desire to change things, no matter the wealth he brings to the table, no matter the advances in technology or the depth of man's wisdom, there are simply times that man's efforts fall short. In moments like these, we bow our heads and cry out to God. God who created the universe. God who spoke the words and all the worlds fell into perfect order. God who breathed life into the tiny, unseen baby floating in your womb. The God who can reverse a desperate situation as easily as He can think a thought or speak a word. We cry out with more emotion than we knew existed within us, and try to find just the right words to move the heart of God. And sometimes, we find that we've cried out to the God who doesn't answer our prayers the way we've begged Him to.

Why did God let your baby die? Why does He let anyone's baby die? Maybe we could understand it better if we knew that He looked down through time and eternity and saw that the miscarried baby would have been left uncared for, so in His mercy He took the child to His home. Maybe if He sat us down and explained His plan to us we could accept His decisions easier. If He showed us that a baby's parents didn't want him or her it wouldn't be so hard to release an unborn baby into eternity's hand. But why *your* baby? The baby you've begged Him for? No doubt you've promised Him your undying devotion to the dying baby you've desired so long. You know He loves you. Surely, He'll show up before it's too late. The grip of love and sorrow tightens as you plead for the life of this baby and wait for God to move.

Then comes the unbelievably horrific report from a physician, or perhaps from your own body: it's all over. No more life. No more chances. No more hope. The baby is gone. What is God thinking? Why didn't He do anything? God, surely you've blown it this time! Your broken heart simply cannot believe that God remains in control. Maybe this is as scary a thought as is the thought of life without this precious continuation of your life and lineage. God not in control? If He cannot save a tiny baby, how can I possibly trust Him with my future and my eternity?

Surely you're not alone. Surely there are others who have questioned God's love and His ability. Could your heart possibly be the only one? There must be those in Scripture who have cried out to a silent sky questioning the Maker of Heaven and Earth. Let's delve into the lives of people who found themselves facing impossible situations and see if God really lost control.

God, Surely You Blew It This Time!
Three Hebrew Boys

"…What god is there who can deliver you out of my hands?"
Shadrach, Meshach and Abednego replied to the king, "O
Nebuchadnezzar, we do not need to give you an answer concerning
this matter. If it be so, our God whom we serve is able to deliver us
from the furnace of blazing fire; and He will deliver us out of your
hand, O king. But even if He does not, let it be known to you, O
king, that we are not going to serve your gods or
worship the golden image that you have set up."
Daniel 3:15-18
"Blessed be the God of Shadrach, Meshach and Abednego,
who has sent His angel and delivered His servants
who put their trust in Him,"
Daniel 3:28

The book of Daniel details a story where it seemed that God had lost control of His universe. We are told that three young men, Shadrach, Meshach and Abednego, were the best and the brightest in the land. The Bible tells us that they were brought from their home in Jerusalem and placed in service to the king. They are described as being youths in whom there was no defect, good-looking, brilliant in all areas, and with uncanny abilities to serve. None was found in the land that could even come close to comparing with these young men. They had their youth, they had their looks, and they had brains! I'll bet there were young women lined up around all the way around the walls of the palace just trying to catch a glimpse of these great catches! They really must have been chosen servants of the most high God! Surely God had His hand on them. Surely nothing bad would happen to them. Right?

In chapter two of Daniel, we see King Nebuchadnezzar tossing and turning all night long. Nightmares were terrifying him and no one could help. God anointed Daniel and he did what no one else in the kingdom could do. He interpreted the king's dream and gave him back his sleep. Because of this, Daniel was given a promotion and placed in a position of honor in the kingdom. One of his first requests as the ruler over the whole province of Babylon was to have Shadrach, Meshach and Abednego appointed over the administration of the province of Babylon. Quite an honor for these young men. Surely God would watch out for them. Surely God wouldn't let heartache come their way. Right?

Chapter three shows the resolve of these young men being greatly tested. They had been forced to leave their home and relocate to Babylon, but God sustained them and even allowed them to assume a place of honor. Everything about them changed—even their names—now their names were synonymous with success and respect. But now they are facing a test greater than any they have ever known. Bow down to a false god, or stand true to the one true God and pay a heavy price.

Shadrach, Meshach and Abednego were ordered by Nebuchadnezzar to bow down and worship a golden image he had created. They had faithfully served God through all areas of their lives. They had no doubt promised to bow their knee to no one other than Jehovah God. Now they have to prove their devotion to their God. And they must prove it with their lives.

Nebuchadnezzar receives word that these young men refuse to worship his idol, and instead have chosen to worship God Almighty and Him alone. How dare they? He'll never stand for this act of rebellion! They embarrass him in full view of the people of Babylon and they expect to suffer no consequences? Nebuchadnezzar flew into a rage of massive proportions. No doubt that even his closest servants dreaded working for him that day! Eyes bulging, face red, sweat pouring, Old King Neb beats his clenched fists on the arms of his throne and stomps his sandaled feet down the halls of the palace and with royal robes flapping in the breeze, ponders the fate of these rebellious young men! But in his fury, he decides to extend a measure of mercy. Because they were such choice men, he offers them a final chance. With this final chance comes a heavy consequence. Bow down and worship or into the furnace you go!

The choice was really no choice at all. Shadrach, Meshach and Abednego made up their minds to worship regardless of the circumstances long before this final confrontation with the king. Even with the king's command to heat the furnace seven times hotter than normal, they were not deterred! It was not enough of a threat to make them bow their knees! They had no worry. They knew God would meet them there.

Imagine the courage it took for these young boys to make their proclamation to the king: *"O Nebuchadnezzar, we do not need to defend ourselves before you in this matter. If we are thrown into the blazing furnace, the God we serve is able to save us from it, and he will rescue us from your hand, O king. But even if he does not, we want you to know, O king, that we will not serve your gods or worship the image of gold you have set up." (Daniel 3:16-18)* What backbone! Staring a mighty king in the face and telling him that he is not enough to force their devotion away from God! Because of this decision to serve God even in the midst of trial, Shadrach, Meshach and Abednego were thrown into a furnace with fire so intense, the soldiers who threw them in perished from the extreme heat.

Those around the throne room that day could easily have decided that God had lost control. Here are three incredible young men standing up for God, yet God allows them to be thrown in the fiery furnace. There's absolutely no way they could survive. God just didn't show up on time, did He? Did He?

Quickly, turn to Daniel chapter three verses 24-25 and look at Nebuchadnezzar's reaction when he so wickedly peered into the flames to watch these young men perish: *Then King Nebuchadnezzar leaped to his feet in amazement and asked his advisers, "Weren't there three men that we tied up and threw into the fire?" They replied,*

"Certainly, O king." He said, "Look! I see four men walking around in the fire, unbound and unharmed, and the fourth looks like a son of the gods." What could have been a tragedy unparalleled in the lives of these young men actually turned out to be their greatest opportunity ever to showcase God's glory and workings in their lives! Without even a singed thread or the smell of smoke, these mighty men of God walked out of the furnace unassisted!

No doubt the death of your baby has been your fiery furnace. You may have wondered if God even knew where you were as you were being cast into the fire of loss. However, just like these three Hebrew boys were never alone for a moment, God walks with you through this heartache. He's standing in the midst of the fire with you. He offers His protection to you, so that you will survive this great sorrow. Even if those around you fall as the soldiers did who threw the boys in the flames, when God stands by your side, your survival is assured. God didn't lose control in that furnace. He hasn't lost control in the furnace of your life, either. A situation where it seems God is a million miles away can become the avenue where you feel the closest to Him. Rather than feeling He's out of control, consider that He is ordering your steps and will use a hurt even this great to bring good to your life and glory to Himself.

Without a doubt, you can be sure that every trial gives you the opportunity to boldly proclaim who our God is! Imagine the cry of the Babylonian people. Who is this God who has saved these three from the fire? Our God! Jehovah God! The greatest threat these Hebrew boys ever faced became their greatest platform for ministry.

When the boys stepped out of the fire, look at what Nebuchadnezzar said: *"Praise be to the God of Shadrach, Meshach and Abednego, who has sent his angel and rescued his servants! They trusted in him and defied the king's command and were willing to give up their lives rather than serve or worship any god except their own God."* (Daniel 3:28) Even in the midst of a great tragedy, you have the opportunity to showcase God's glory. Someone will see God in your life, because they see Him bring you through a trial. When you stand on the other side of heartache, and boldly proclaim that because of

God you have survived the heartache of the death of your baby, someone will see and their life will be changed.

The struggle you are facing is very much like the fiery furnace these heroic young men faced. You have a great decision in front of you, and the choices you make will likely affect the remainder of your days on this planet—and the heat is on! You must decide whether you will bow your knee to the sorrow, hurt and anger that strives to consume the heart of the childless parent who has unwillingly released their baby into eternity's hand. Will you allow the flames of anger to annihilate your heart and your relationships? Will you stand helplessly as the heat of the battle melts you like wax as you face the fires of sorrow and empty arms? Will the hurt that permeates every fiber of your being disintegrate you to nothing more than a pile of burned up ashes?

"But these are not choices," you cry. "I would never choose to have my baby die! I would never choose to hurt this badly!" No, you never would make these horrible, hurtful choices if these were the choices you had been given. But now you stand at the crossroads of your existence and you do have choices to make. Will you remain paralyzed in fear and pain and allow the fire of this trial to consume you or will you take the hand of the Savior who has promised to stand with you in the fire and come forth as pure gold?

The fire is inevitable. You simply cannot escape feelings of hurt and disappointment following the death of a precious baby. Your emotions may be more intense than some or less devastating than others, but the fact remains that you cannot survive the death of your child unscathed. The fire is there. But God has promised that you do not have to face this fire alone.

Isaiah 43:2b-3a says *"When you walk through the fire, you will not be burned; the flames will not set you ablaze. For I am the LORD, your God, the Holy One of Israel, your Savior"*. I want you to notice a single, yet very powerful and encouraging word in this passage of Scripture. Only four short letters. It's the word *"when"*. What's the big deal about the world *"when"*? It doesn't really mean anything, does it? Oh yes, my friend, it does! *When* you walk through the fire...not *if* you walk through the fire. **When!** You are guaranteed to have to face the fire sometime in your life! It's written right there in black and white! **When** you walk through the fire. Do you realize what this powerful, little four letter word is saying to you? It is saying to you that God, in His infinite wisdom, knew before the foundations of the world that you would face this fire. He knew that you would stand with your toes touching the hot, burning surface of the furnace, the tears stinging your eyes like the heat of the flames stings your skin. He knew the very moment when you would tumble heart first into the fires. He knew that the trials of heartache would lick at your heart like flames licking kindling. This problem that may have blindsided you never even caused God to flinch. All of this assurance wrapped up in one tiny, little four-letter word: *when.*

Okay. That explains how the word "when" is powerful, but how in the world could this possibly be encouraging? It sure doesn't excite my heart to know that the embers are glowing somewhere in the future of my existence! How could it possibly help me to know that God knew the fire was coming? Simple! Since God already knew the fire was coming, He knew where to stand when the sparks started to fly! Just as He did for Shadrach, Meshach and Abednego, God stands in the midst of the flames with you. He doesn't come running to sweep up the ashes after you have been destroyed. He doesn't stand on the outside of the furnace wringing His holy, yet helpless hands. No! He chooses to walk unflinchingly through the opening of the furnace and promises to stand there with you.

Perhaps you were blessed with wonderful friends who stood beside you when the tone of your conversation turned from jubilation to sorrow. Or maybe it was understanding family members who supported you when the atmosphere was so heavy with grief that you could hardly stand. But as much as godly friends and family would love to stay with you through every step of your hurt, and would give any of their earthly possessions to remove the searing pain in your heart, they can only do so much and go so far. They can stand with you to best of their ability, and thank God for their willingness to do so. But they are mere mortals and can only do so much as you are enveloped in the inferno of miscarriage or stillbirth.

But child of God, look at your Father's assurance to you: *"you will not be burned; the flames will not set you ablaze."* Friend, God does more than simply plan ahead and know when your trials are coming. And even though His presence with you in the fire is an incredible gift, it simply is not enough for God! He promises you this: you will not be burned! The flames will not set you ablaze! This is not to say that the heat will not be seven times hotter than anything you've ever known, but because God is who He says He is—*your Lord, the God of Israel*—you have an eternal assurance that the fires will not consume you, no matter how hot. No matter how dark. No matter how scary. God is telling you here that He will allow the trial but He will not allow you to be destroyed!

Do you realize that God never intended for you to remain in the furnace of grief forever? If you could travel to ancient Babylon and find the exact furnace in this account, you simply would not find the ashes of these godly young men. You could search forever and not find traces of them anywhere. God walked with them through the flames, and He led them out of the furnace as well.

You may believe that since the death of your baby you will never be truly happy again. You may be convinced that sorrow will be your closest companion and grief now defines who you are. What would have happened if Shadrach, Meshach and Abednego had refused to walk out of the kiln and instead stayed in the fire longer than they had to? When the fourth Man stepped forward and said "Come on boys. It's time to go," how foolish would they have been to dig their heels in and refuse to leave? "No God, I think I'll stay here a little longer. I'm just not ready to face the world of the unflamed." Can you imagine the absurdity of that choice?

I can almost hear you now: "That's stupid! I hate feeling this way! I'd do anything to lay these hurtful feelings down!" Perhaps you have found the hottest flames in the fire to be the flames of anger. You may even feel anger rising up in you as I suggest that some become stuck in the furnace of anger. No one wants to reside in anger and bitterness but for some, the anger becomes the familiar, and the familiar is sometimes not as scary as the unknown so the furnace becomes home. Perhaps you are afraid that rising up from the ashes of anger means you are betraying the baby you were never allowed to raise. Leaving the furnace behind feels like you're leaving behind your only tie to your baby. Nothing could be further from the truth.

Friend, please realize that anger is not a sin. Ephesians 4:26 says "*In your anger, do not sin*", but it goes further and says "*Do not let the sun go down while you are still angry*" (NIV). God knows you will feel anger during different seasons of your life. Your emotions don't scare God or throw Him off track. He is the very One who planted your emotions deep down inside of you when He created you in His image and His likeness. However, anger left unresolved will spread across the dry, barren places of your soul like wildfire. Spiritually, you'll look like the fires that spread uncontrollably across dry prairies in the summer time with the flames destroying everything in their paths. We are warned over and over again in Scripture not to let anger take root in our hearts. Be slow to anger. Get rid of all bitterness, rage and anger. (Ephesians 4:31 NIV) James 1:19-20 says that the anger of man does not bring about the righteous life that God desires. If you allow your anger to consume you, you'll never be able to achieve the things God has laid out for you in His perfect plan for your life. Remember that the same Holy God who tells you that anger is not a sin is the same God who tells you that you must surrender the anger to the flames and trusting Him completely, take His hand and allow Him to lead you out of the furnace.

If the Hebrew boys had stayed in the flames when God stepped out, they would have been annihilated and utterly destroyed. His presence in that furnace that day assured them that they were safe and secure. They were in His care and no weapon formed against them—not the threats of the king, not the flames of the furnace—would prosper. The same God they trusted to walk with them through the fire was the same God they trusted to lead them out of the fire! He remains that trustworthy today as you experience the fires of miscarriage!

So what do you do when the anger wells up inside of you so that you begin to fear the person you are becoming? How do you lay it down and walk out of the furnace? The answer is found in Colossians 3:15: *"Let the peace of Christ rule in your hearts"*. There's an amazing little nugget of truth for you here. The original meaning for the word "rule" here is awesome, especially for sports fans! It literally means "to act as an umpire"! With your permission, the peace of Christ will act as an umpire when anger and calm wage war within you!

Imagine a sporting event with no referees. Athletes have prepared their bodies and their game plans, the spectators are in the stands and the popcorn has been popped! Halfway through the game a controversial play is made and the athletes are at each other's throats! What would happen if there were no men in pseudo-fashionable black and white striped shirts to step between these mammoth men and decide who would prevail? The players would get so angry over the play that they would lash out against each other, kicking teammates instead of the ball. End zones would remain vacant. Baskets would hang still. Nets would sit silent. All as capable, well-trained athletes get so caught up in fury that no one notices balls rolling past sidelines and frustrated spectators leaving the stands. There is no one to referee and bring peace to the situation. Anger would cause the game to be void. Just like your heart.

When anger rears its ugly head let the peace of God rule. You'll notice that a few moments ago, I said the peace of Christ would rule *with your permission*. The very first word of that verse is "let". You must *let* the peace of Christ rule. Jesus Christ is quite the gentleman and He will not force His way into your heart, but oh, the peace that He brings when you invite Him in and allow Him to do His work. Just as an umpire steps between two raging, muscle-bound men on a football field, Christ will step in between anger and calm and send the enemy of your soul to the sidelines. Referees at sporting events bring their yellow flags to halt the action when an offense has been made. Jesus brings with Him peace that passes all understanding. He grants peace that just doesn't make sense considering the situation you're in. Peace in the midst of miscarriage. Calm in the time of grief. Commit your struggle with anger to the same God who walked with Shadrach, Meshach and Abednego through the flames. You'll find that you will be the victor in this contest against anger.

Don't believe it? Ask Shadrach. He'll probably invite you to smell his hair! You won't smell smoke! Talk to Abednego. Ask him to show you his scars. You'll probably see a quizzical look on his face! He really won't know what you're talking about! And Meshach? He'll probably tell you what it was like to count three others beside himself strolling through fire that day. God walked with them through their furnace. What makes you think He'll abandon you in yours?

61

God, Surely You Blew It This Time!
Lazarus

❧

[1]*Now a certain man was sick, Lazarus of Bethany, the village of Mary and her sister Martha.* [2]*It was the Mary who anointed the Lord with ointment, and wiped His feet with her hair, whose brother Lazarus was sick.* [3]*So the sisters sent word to Him, saying, "Lord, behold, he whom You love is sick."* [4]*But when Jesus heard this, He said, "This sickness is not to end in death, but for the glory of God, so that the Son of God may be glorified by it."* [5]*Now Jesus loved Martha and her sister and Lazarus.* [6]*So when He heard that he was sick, He then stayed two days longer in the place where He was.* [11]*This He said, and after that He said to them, "Our friend Lazarus has fallen asleep; but go, so that I may awaken him out of sleep."* [12]*The disciples then said to Him, "Lord, if he has fallen asleep, he will recover."* [13]*Now Jesus had spoken of his death, but they thought that He was speaking of literal sleep.* [14]*So Jesus then said to them plainly, "Lazarus is dead,* [15]*and I am glad for your sakes that I was not there, so that you may believe; but let us go to him."* [17]*So when Jesus came, He found that he had already been in the tomb four days.* [18]*Now Bethany was near Jerusalem, about two miles off;* [19]*and many of the Jews had come to Martha and Mary, to console them concerning their brother.* [20]*Martha therefore, when she heard that Jesus was coming, went to meet Him, but Mary*

stayed at the house. *²¹Martha then said to Jesus, "Lord, if You had been here, my brother would not have died. ²²"Even now I know that whatever You ask of God, God will give You." ²³Jesus said to her, "Your brother will rise again."³⁰Now Jesus had not yet come into the village, but was still in the place where Martha met Him. ³¹Then the Jews who were with her in the house, and consoling her, when they saw that Mary got up quickly and went out, they followed her, supposing that she was going to the tomb to weep there. ³²Therefore, when Mary came where Jesus was, she saw Him, and fell at His feet, saying to Him, "Lord, if You had been here, my brother would not have died." ³³When Jesus therefore saw her weeping, and the Jews who came with her also weeping, He was deeply moved in spirit and was troubled, ³⁴and said, "Where have you laid him?" They said to Him, "Lord, come and see." ³⁵Jesus wept. ³⁶So the Jews were saying, "See how He loved him!" ³⁷But some of them said, "Could not this man, who opened the eyes of the blind man, have kept this man also from dying?" ³⁸So Jesus, again being deeply moved within, came to the tomb. Now it was a cave, and a stone was lying against it. ³⁹Jesus said, "Remove the stone." Martha, the sister of the deceased, said to Him, "Lord, by this time there will be a stench, for he has been dead four days." ⁴⁰Jesus said to her, "Did I not say to you that if you believe, you will see the glory of God?" ⁴¹So they removed the stone. Then Jesus raised His eyes, and said, "Father, I thank You that You have heard Me. ⁴²"I knew that You always hear Me; but because of the people standing around I said it, so that they may believe that You sent Me." ⁴³When He had said these things, He cried out with a loud voice, "Lazarus, come forth." ⁴⁴The man who had died came forth, bound hand and foot with wrappings, and his face was wrapped around with a cloth. Jesus said to them, "Unbind him, and let him go." ⁴⁵Therefore many of the Jews who came to Mary, and saw what He had done, believed in Him.*
John 11:1-6, 11-15, 17-23, 30-45

This passage of Scripture in John 11 lets us in on an incredibly intense time in the lives of some very close friends of Jesus. Mary, Martha and Lazarus were some of the closest earthly friends Jesus had outside of His disciples. They supported His ministry, provided food for Him, and Mary is even the Mary mentioned in Scripture as having poured her oil on Jesus' feet then drying them with her hair in an incredible public outpouring of love and affection for her Master. One would think that these folks on the "inside track" would be able to call in a few favors from Jesus when problems rose. One would think.

God's silence is confusing to many Christians, even those who have served God faithfully their entire lives. You believe God will move on your behalf. You know He can. You're just waiting. And waiting. Surely He'll move before it's too late. "But, God! It *is* too late!" You've served Him faithfully for years, yet He seems to turn a deaf ear to your pleas to save your baby. Why? Doesn't He love me anymore? Doesn't He know what's going on? If these questions haunt you, keep reading. You'll find some answers in the story of Lazarus.

One day, Lazarus became very ill. Not just the sniffles or a pesky cough. An illness so severe that it became obvious to everyone around that he would die. Perhaps like your miscarriage. Not just some queasiness. Not a little spotting. But a condition so terrifying that not even science or good genes could intercept the tragedy headed for your door.

Mary and Martha did what any of us who had witnessed God in the flesh would have done. They called on Jesus. I can just hear them—can't you? "Mary, Lazarus looks terrible! He's burning up with a fever, and he's so delirious he thinks he's in Bethlehem! I'll find fresh water to cool him, and you get word to Jesus." "Of course, Martha! We'll find Jesus. I know He'll help us. He's so very good to us, you know. And how He loves Lazarus! I'll send word to Him right away. Don't you worry, brother! Jesus will be here as soon as He finds out you're sick! Then everything will be okay."

Why do we pretend to understand God? His mind is so incredibly complex that there is simply no way our humanity could fathom His plan. Mary and Martha "knew" that once Jesus heard Lazarus was deathly ill, He'd drop what He was doing and come right away. One Word from His lips and any sign of death or disease would cease to exist. What happened? Did someone forget to tell Jesus? No. Look at verses 3 and 4 of John chapter 11: *So the sisters sent word to Him, saying, "Lord, behold, he whom You love is sick." But when Jesus heard this...*

The word got to the Word. Someone pushed through the crowd, sweaty from the mini-marathon he'd just run, and breathlessly told Jesus "Lord, the one you love is sick!" I can just see this messenger instantly turn on a dime and take off running in the same direction from which he has traveled. He's not going to miss this miracle! Jesus raising up a man so weak he can't even lift his own head? It will be something to tell his children about! After only a few yards, he realizes Jesus is not behind him. Imagine the cloud of dust as he puts on the brakes! "Jesus! It's Lazarus! *Lazarus!* Your friend! He's *dying*! You've got to come and You've got to come <u>*now*</u>!" He turns to run again, expecting Jesus' expression to change to one of realization and His posture to change from standing to running. But Jesus didn't come. Imagine the confused messenger as he faced the daunting task of telling Mary and Martha that Jesus had stayed put!

So what was Jesus thinking? Did He not care about Lazarus? Nothing could be further from the truth. Go back to verse 3 again: *"The one whom You love is sick."* Maybe Martha had upset Jesus by being too busy for the important things of life, and He decided that this was what she deserved. Not a chance. Check out verse 5: *Now Jesus loved Martha and her sister and Lazarus.* What was He thinking? Maybe He was so far away that Lazarus died before Jesus could get there. Guess again! Bethany was only two miles from Jerusalem. Jesus was no doubt in great physical shape. He could've gotten there in thirty minutes if He took His time. Instead, He waited. And waited. And waited.

We know that Jesus waited at least six days before He showed up at the home of Mary and Martha. Six days! Verse 6 tells us that Jesus waited where He was for two days after He was told that Lazarus was sick, and verse 17 tells us that Lazarus had been in the tomb four whole days when Jesus finally sauntered on the scene! For two whole days, He stayed put. I wonder what He was doing?

Did He play with children? Did He fish with the disciples? Did He nap under a fig tree? Whatever He did or didn't do, it had to seem to everyone around Him that He had finally blown it!

After two days passed, Jesus finally decided it was the right time to move. You could almost hear that collective sigh of relief from His buddies. "Whew! Lazarus should be fine now!" Then Jesus delivered the bombshell: "Lazarus is asleep." The brilliant, yet blinded followers of Jesus didn't get it. "Oh! Is that all! Well, fellas, let's go wake him up!" They were actually the ones who needed to be woken up! "No. Lazarus is dead." No sugarcoating this message. Lazarus didn't make it. Jesus had been perfection in the flesh, but somehow, for whatever reason, Jesus really must have messed up this time! Or so it seemed. It may have looked like Jesus wasn't doing anything to help these precious people He loved so much, and who loved Him in return. On the contrary, Jesus was simply laying the groundwork for the greatest miracle of Lazarus' life! For you see, the illness defeated life, but it could not defeat *Life*.

What Jesus told His followers when He told them that Lazarus had died simply blows me away. I would love to have seen the expression on the faces of those around Him when He said *"Lazarus is dead, and I am glad for your sakes that I was not there, so that you may believe;"* What? You're **glad?** One of Your best friends just died and You tell me that You are **glad** that You were not there to stop it?

Jesus' explanation must not have made any sense to them either. He wanted them to believe. Believe what? That He had lost control? That He didn't care about people anymore? That death was too strong an opponent for Him? Not on your life! As great a miracle as it would have been for Jesus to raise Lazarus up from some horrible disease, it was a greater miracle to raise him from the grave. It's an even greater miracle when a heart crushed and broken can somehow find a way to believe in a God that doesn't always make sense. Jesus had a far greater plan for this family. He has a far greater plan for yours!

Jesus had finally decided the time was right to come. Martha could not contain herself any longer, and had to have an explanation for His delay. Mary stayed at home, probably comforting her parents or putting her arm around those who loved her brother. But not Martha! Good old, confrontational Martha! She's gotta know what happened! She ran to meet Jesus saying, "Oh, Jesus! If you had just been here!"

I wonder if she asked Him why He wasn't there. Have you? "God, why weren't You there when I needed You most? Where were You when my baby died? Why didn't You help the doctors know what to do? Why won't You tell me what to do?" Are you beginning to feel like a modern day Martha? Keep going. Perhaps you'll find a way to connect with Martha's heart even more.

Martha didn't stop when she told Jesus she knew He could have helped. She kept going. Good old Martha! *"Even now I know that whatever You ask of God, God will give You."* I love those first two words...**_Even now!_** Even now that the one I love is dead, *even now* that it seems that You've ignored our cries for help and mercy, *even now* that I'm so broken inside that I simply don't know how I'll face tomorrow, *even now I know that whatever you ask of God, He'll give to You.*

Somehow, though blinded by her tears, Martha found a precious measure of faith. She stands looking eye to eye with God robed in human flesh. The God who created Lazarus' body, yet for whatever reason, refused to recreate it. No excuses. Nothing to hide behind. Just a face-to-face encounter with a God who said "No." Martha could have cursed Him. She could have told Him that He was cruel. She could have turned her back on Him, walked away and never looked back. Thank God she didn't! She simply said, come what may, I know You are still able. My circumstances are screaming out at me that You've surely blown it this time. This horrible situation says that my family slipped through the proverbial cracks. My emotions may not be in line with what I proclaim to You today, but somehow, *even now,* I know You're still God and You're still in charge.

You have the same choice to make as Martha had that day. You can curse God and walk away from Him, refusing to believe in a God who refused to spare the life of your baby. God allows you to make that choice for yourself. You can wrap yourself so tightly around your hurt that no one is allowed in. Or you can choose to trust in an unseen God whose plan is more invisible than His face. *Even now* I trust You. *Even now* that my baby has died, *even now* that we are having trouble conceiving again, *even now* that my heart still hurts and the tears still flow, I know You are still God and You still have a plan for my life.

How did Martha find this faith to believe in Jesus? This same Jesus who has disappointed her? Read verse 27 of John 11: "*She said to Him, 'Yes, Lord; I have believed that You are the Christ, the Son of God...*" When everything in her life was total chaos, when nothing made sense—even her relationship with God, she still chose to believe that Jesus really was who He said He was. She believed through her hurt and tears that Jesus really was God in the flesh; He was the Messiah, the Son of God. Once that realization became as solid as concrete, all other problems began to resolve. Yes, the hurt was still there. Lazarus was still dead. Mary was still weeping. But Martha grabbed hold of the reality of who Jesus was, and part of her world began to make sense again.

Following the death of a baby, nothing makes sense at all. We know that everyone has to die someday. But when a baby dies before it hardly has a chance to live, the world seems to have been turned upside down. One desperate mother who found herself wrapped in profound grief following the loss of her baby told me that she simply could not pray anymore. Her heart hurt too much. The praise that had once so freely poured from her lips was now replaced with oceans of tears. She felt like God wouldn't listen anyway. He refused to listen when she begged Him to spare the life of her child. Why would He listen to her now?

If this is the broken cry of your heart, allow me to remind you of something. When God seems silent, He is still there and He is still working and moving on your behalf. He has taken every tear you've ever cried and He keeps them in a bottle (Psalm 56:8). He is never disinterested in your hurt and will never scoff at your pain. If it feels like you've been abandoned by God, please keep reading the story of Lazarus and his sisters.

Jesus' next interaction was with Mary. Martha runs home and brings Mary back to Jesus. When Mary sees the Lord, she falls at His feet and says the same thing Martha has said: "Oh, Jesus! If

You'd only been here, Lazarus wouldn't have died!" Can't you see Mary? Weeping at the feet of Jesus now. One day she'll fall at these same feet overcome with adoration rather than sorrow. But today her heart is destroyed because she felt like Jesus didn't come when she needed Him.

Did Jesus stop loving Mary and Martha? How could He stand to see such pain when He clearly had the ability to stop it? If you've ever doubted that Jesus loves you, if you've ever wondered how to believe that He feels the same pain you feel, allow me to point you to a profound passage of Scripture. It is found in John 11:35. It says simply *"Jesus wept."*

I believe Jesus was highly emotional. When you love deeply, you grieve deeply. That's why the death of your baby has been so difficult for you to survive. When Scripture says that Jesus wept, I believe He did just that. I don't believe His eyes just teared up. I do not believe that a solitary tear trickled down His leathery face. I believe He did what the Bible tells us He did. He wept! Tears must have flowed in abundance that day! The very heart that originated love was now being torn in two! The Prince of Peace wrapped in the embrace of love and sorrow? Why weep when He knew what was about to happen? He knew that in a matter of moments, He was going to raise Lazarus from the grave and that there would be a massive celebration. Yet, now He weeps. Why?

The answer is actually quite simple. You can read it for yourself in John 11:33:

> *"When Jesus saw her weeping, and the Jews who*
> *had come along with her also weeping, he was deeply*
> *moved in spirit and troubled."*

Jesus was hurting because those He loved were hurting. That's all there is to it! He wasn't sad because Lazarus died! He knew that Lazarus' death sentence was about to be pardoned! He wasn't crying because He felt helpless or hopeless! He held the power of life and death in His hands, yet today He held His own face in His hands and cried! He cried tears of sorrow because Mary and Martha and their friends cried tears of sorrow. Jesus very simply felt the same feelings they did that day, wrapped His arms around them and wept.

How many nights since you've experienced the horror of miscarriage or stillbirth have you cried yourself to sleep? When you lost your baby, did you lose your joy? Know that in these sad moments, the Son of God bows His head and weeps with you. Just like He did with Mary and Martha, He comes alongside you, wraps His arms tightly around you, and His tears flow like yours.

As you weep, remember another similarity in your story and theirs. Even though Christ weeps with you, He still knows the end of the story! Your baby's life didn't end when your baby's body died. Even though your baby now lives in a different realm of reality than we do, your baby is so very much alive! God loves you enough to provide a means for you to be forever reunited with this baby you have loved and lost! Christ knows that! He was the provision! Just like He knew Lazarus would be raised from the grave, He knows that your baby lives forevermore in Heaven, eternally in a place of perfection, and that your baby is waiting for your arrival! Oh, what a reunion that will be!

Go back with me for a moment to Lazarus' tomb. After Jesus has wept with Lazarus' family, He knows it's time for the main event. Jesus takes a deep breath, and with a voice that must have pealed throughout time and eternity, Jesus cried "Lazarus! Come forth!" (It's a good thing Jesus actually said Lazarus' name! Every dead body from the beginning of time may have come stumbling out of their graves that day!) Can you imagine the looks on Mary and Martha's faces? They knew Jesus could do anything, but now they are seeing that proof with their own eyes! They have warned Jesus that Lazarus had been dead so long that he stunk, but now this brother is hobbling out of his grave! Tightly bound in grave clothes and head covered, Lazarus walks out of that tomb very much alive! Probably very much confused as well, but very much alive! (Did you ever wonder if Lazarus wondered what was going on?)

Picture the looks on everyone's faces! I see Martha with absolute shock on her face. I see Mary as her knees buckle and the tears begin to flow. I see Jesus' eyes twinkling with a huge smile spreading across His face. Hear the gasps? That's Mary & Martha! Hear that hearty laugh? That's Jesus! He wept freely with those who have wept, and now He rejoices just as freely!

Oh, the jubilation that went on that day! Mary & Martha reunited with the brother snatched away by that vicious enemy, Death. Singing, dancing, hugging, kissing! It had to go on well into the night! Great sorrow turned to greater joy! I don't know what all they did that night, but of one thing I am sure. I believe Jesus was right in the middle of it! I believe He sang! I believe He kicked up His heels! I believe He grabbed Lazarus and hugged him so tight that his feet came up off the ground!

Now imagine your upcoming family reunion! I'm not talking about a family gathering in the middle of the summer where all your aunts kiss you and leave lipstick marks on your cheeks! I'm talking about the moment where you will be eternally reunited with the baby taken from you too early. Imagine the look on your face. Imagine the look on your spouse's face. How will you respond? Don't know? That's okay. If you are a Christian, you *will* know! Because for the Christian, that day is coming! Imagine the joy on the face of your child! They've waited a long time for you too! What a glorious party! All that sorrow suddenly transformed into unbelievable portions of joy! Together again! No separation! Not now—not ever!

Imagine what it will feel like to touch his or her hair! Won't it be wonderful to stroke your child's face? But if you can tear your eyes away from the face of that son or daughter for just a second, glance at the face of Jesus. I'll bet His eyes are twinkling! You may just find yourself wrapped in His arms and feel your feet being lifted off the ground!

What was the greatest joy of the day Lazarus was raised from the dead? Was it that Mary and Martha had their brother back? Was it that Lazarus had a second chance to do all that he wanted to do with his life? The greatest joy of the day was that God received the glory for what Jesus had done. The players involved could have chosen to proclaim to anyone who was listening that Jesus really messed up this time. He came with too little too late. Rather, they chose to believe and God received glory from a horrific situation. What an honor for the members of this family!

As tragic as your situation is, you have an opportunity to give God glory through your pain. The choice is laid before you today: turn to God with all your hurt and all your frustration, and let Him carry it for you, or turn your back on Him and run. What do you believe? That God is not really in control? After all, He apparently could not save even one innocent little baby. Or do you believe that He is still working a mighty plan, even though your eyes and your mind cannot fathom what He is doing? The choice, my friend, is yours.

God, Surely You Blew It This Time!
Calvary

∽✐∼

As we consider situations where it had to seem that God messed up, that He had lost complete control, let's look at one more story. Picture this scenario. A large crowd gathers to participate in an exciting turn of events. People are saying that it's about time *somebody* got to that man! He was wreaking havoc on this society! Son of *God*? Surely He didn't really expect us to believe that? After all, He was just the boy of some carpenter. You'd think His father would have taught Him to tell the truth.

The disciples had watched Jesus for a few years at this point. They witnessed with their very own eyes how He had turned water into wine and saved a nervous bridegroom from a lifetime of embarrassment. No one had to tell them how He had walked on the water—Peter walked with Him. There was no confusion about how He drove the demons from the madman of Gerasenes and returned him to his family. No, they watched the man's twisted, grotesque features melt into the face of a compassionate man overwhelmed with gratitude for the transformation brought about by Jesus' mere words. And no one could forget watching the widow's son hop up out of his coffin and begin to talk! They remembered everything about that day—the son jabbering, the crowd gasping, the mother dropping to her knees, overcome with emotion when Jesus gave her back her son. They remembered everything Jesus did. They remembered His preaching,

His teaching. They remember His confronting the important religious leaders of the day. But they simply could not remember a time when Jesus failed.

Now some of these same men stand perplexed in the shadow of a cruel tree that would soon become Jesus' execution station. The events of the last several hours have left them perplexed. Shattered. Confused. All He was doing was praying. He wasn't threatening anyone. He wasn't causing a disturbance. But they came with torches to arrest the Light of the World, and used violence to capture the Prince of Peace? Unbelievable! Terror gripped His friends tighter than any vice in any carpenter shop in the land, and they ran. After all, Jesus can handle it. He'll not allow them to arrest Him. Surely He wouldn't let something this horrible happen. Surely.

He will do something. Won't He? He'll say some mind-blowing truth and Herod will let Him go. Right? Jesus! Why the silence? Now is the time you *have* to speak! They're accusing You, Jesus! Make it stop! Everyone knows You can—but no one knows why You won't! Oh, Jesus, could it be that You're really messing up this time?

The friends are gone. Peter has even cursed the Name of the One He promised to eternally defend. Jesus, Your confidants deserted you. They just didn't understand. Why didn't you make them help You? Couldn't You do something? Why *wouldn't* You do something?

A scourging? Surely not! He'll have to do something now! Just watch! He'll surely call down fire from Heaven before the cat of nine tails comes down on His back. He'll slay that soldier for even thinking of causing Him pain. Won't He? But again and again, His flesh is beaten until it hangs like ribbons and His intestines are exposed. How can He shed this much blood and still live? Jesus! *Do something!* This hurts too much! God, make them stop! Please! Your Child is dying! Why are You silent still? Why are You turning Your head from this need? Oh, God, this simply cannot be in Your plan! Surely You've messed up this time.

A cross? A crucifixion? Not for Jesus! He's been in the business of restoring life to the dead, not dying Himself! Wasn't the pain of His beating enough? How much hurt, how much destruction does He have to face before You'll step in? But You'll step in now, won't You, God? You won't really watch Your Child die without intervening. You love Him too much to allow His death. Don't You? Oh, God! How can You bear it! How can You survive the loss of One You love so much? Even You? You *are* still in control... *aren't You?*

They're laying nails on the ground now, God! By His hands and His feet! God, don't You know what they're planning to do? Stop them! Can't You? Why won't You? Don't let them destroy the hands that brought life back to the widow's son, the feet that walked on water! God, He is so good. He is so kind! He is so innocent! He doesn't deserve this! What are You thinking? God, have You lost control this time?

Jesus cannot die. Not Jesus! He waits until the last minute sometimes, but He always comes through in the end. It will take some time for Him to recover from His injuries, but He'll come down off that cross and then everyone will see how powerful and mighty God is. Right? He's coming down alive, right? Please, Jesus. Do something. Don't let this horrible thing happen. Don't let death conquer You! Not You, Jesus. Not You.

Could there ever be an experience more surreal than standing at the grave of Jesus? How can the witnesses of so many miracles believe He's really dead? Knowing what they know about Him. Seeing what they've seen. Feeling what they've felt. But now, everything they've ever held as true is overshadowed by the size of the stone covering the opening to His tomb. Every belief questioned. Every foundation crumbling. God's silence is louder than the mightiest storm or trumpet blast. Where was God when He was so desperately needed? Didn't He know what was going on? Didn't He care? Didn't He know what to do? God, surely You blew it this time.

The people who watched Jesus die must surely have thought that God had failed. Everything up to this point had been wonderful, exciting, and life changing. But apparently, Jesus' time on earth was over. He was an incredible, charismatic man, but evidently that's all He was. A man. Not the Son of God that He proclaimed Himself to be.

Jump ahead in the story a few days. Do you remember what happened? Sure you do! With unparalleled authority, God Almighty used every power at His disposal and brought Jesus Christ forth from the grave triumphant over death and hell! Death didn't conquer Christ! Not by a long shot! Death must bow down to Life at His command! Hell trembles and falls powerless at the sound of His Name! What appeared to be Heaven's greatest defeat was in reality Heaven's greatest conquest! Because of Christ's sacrifice on Calvary, you and I are given access to the throne room of Heaven! Sin is defeated and Satan cannot hold you captive any more! Because of Jesus' sacrificial death and His mighty resurrection, we can be reconciled to our Father! Because of this sacrifice, you can be eternally reunited with the baby you've carried in your heart so much longer than in your womb.

Perhaps as you struggle with the death of your baby, you wonder why God is silent. Why didn't God intervene and save your baby's life? You knew He could. You just know that He didn't. It may seem like God has betrayed you, that perhaps He abandoned you like Jesus' friends abandoned Him in the Garden of Gethsemane. Friend, nothing could be further from the truth. Calvary seemed like a great mistake to those who loved the Lord. I'm certain they expected God to break through with lightning bolts from Heaven and slay those who were killing His Child. When He didn't, can you imagine their confusion? Why would God let His Child die, and do nothing? Why would God let *your* child die, and do nothing?

Looking back at Calvary, we see that God had a greater plan than the people of the day realized. God's heart was breaking! God loves with an intensity that we simply cannot comprehend. He certainly didn't want to see His Child suffer. He doesn't sit on His throne with a cruel heart enjoying the suffering of His children. He doesn't enjoy your suffering any more than He did Jesus'. But God knew that innocent Jesus had to die to redeem us from our sins. Remember that in the Garden of Gethsemane, Jesus begged His Father to take this cup away from Him—to find another way. Jesus knew the cup He had to drink and He knew it would be bitter. Jesus also knew that the Father's plan was the only way to redeem your sins and mine, and allow us a way to be reconciled to the Father. Therefore, in an abundance of love for you, Jesus submitted to the will of His Father. Gethsemane is a heart-wrenching portrait of a Child begging the Father to remove suffering, yet God in His infinite wisdom and love—yes, *love*—said "No".

God had to remember this plea as the torture of His Baby was being carried out. Jesus didn't politely ask God to find another way. Did the sound of Jesus weeping ring in God's ears as the sounds of the pounding of the nails rang through the streets of Jerusalem? He was fighting a greater battle than any of us will ever face. So distraught was Jesus over the knowledge of what the hours ahead would hold that He literally began to sweat blood, a rare medical condition called hematidrosis. The capillaries beneath the surface of His skin ruptured under the level of stress He was enduring as He faced His ultimate sacrifice. This is how hard Jesus was pleading with God. This is how broken Christ's heart was that day. Surely, Jesus knows how to identify with the brokenness of your heart.

God the Father heard the cries of His only begotten Son that horrible night in Gethsemane. Yet He held back His tears and He held back His hand and allowed the slaughter of His one and only Son to proceed.

Can you imagine voluntarily giving your child up for slaughter for the sake of someone else? Can you fathom being able to stop His death, but choosing not to, all for the love of people who had yet to be born? Some would love Him and live for Him. Some would turn their backs on Him. Some would curse His Name. Yet the love of the Father is the same for all.

A woman named Erin was thrilled to learn she was pregnant. A baby was on the way! What an exciting future was ahead! When she went for her first ultrasound appointment expecting to see the flicker of a tiny heartbeat, Erin received the news that no Mother wants to hear. Instead of finding a heartbeat, her own heart began to break as she found herself facing the devastating diagnosis of miscarriage. To further deepen her sorrow, as the physician continued the exam, she indifferently mentioned the presence of a twin, also with the absence of a heartbeat. Rather than experiencing the joy of seeing proof of life within her womb, Erin found herself face to face with the death of not one, but two of her precious babies. Following her loss, Erin decided to name her babies Song and Treasure based on the comfort she found in Matthew 6:20 and Psalm 40:3.

In the time following her miscarriage, Erin's faith was shaken. Sorrow such as this has a tendency to wreak havoc on the heart. However, Erin found a beautiful truth through her tragedy. This is how she sums it all up: "The loss of my babies actually makes me more in awe of God, for willingly giving His only Son, for me, to pay for my sin. I think I can appreciate that more now that I know how tightly I held on to my children, never even knowing them." What a fantastic truth! As earthly Mothers and Fathers, we would do anything in our power to save our baby. Medicines, surgery, bed rest. Whatever the doctor orders. Anything to save this baby. We hold on so tightly to tiny little people we've never even laid our eyes on because we already love them so very deeply. The grip of love tightens a little more.

But to think that God loved us enough to let go of His Child! To willingly give His Child for me! And to think that Jesus willingly gave Himself! You know the love you have for the baby you have lost. Imagine the love God has for you, to allow His Baby to die in your place! How great is the love the Father has lavished on us, that we should be called children of God! (1 John 3:1)

Was Calvary a mistake? Did God mess up? Do ministers just try to put a positive spin on the story so you'll continue attending church in an attempt to resolve some measure of guilt? Nothing could be further from the truth. God had a greater plan for humanity and the only way to reconcile you with Him was the sacrificial death of Jesus Christ. Even in the darkest moments, when it seemed like all was lost, God was in complete and totally loving control. Not one moment, not even one millisecond of that day was lost to God. He orchestrated each and every event. And He did it all for you.

Following the death of a baby, there may be times that the Lord's apparent absence can be terrifying. You can't hear Him. You can't feel Him. You find yourself questioning everything you've ever believed about Him. The reality is that even at your darkest moment when He seems the most silent, He is still interceding for you to the Father. "Father, these are my children. The ones I died for. They're hurting.

Send the Holy Spirit to comfort them." And with the compassion of a loving Father, God does the work.

Your heart cries out that your baby didn't deserve to die. God understands. His Baby didn't deserve to die either. But if your baby can take part in bringing Glory to the Almighty Creator of Heaven and Earth, what greater honor could ever be bestowed upon that child? Fulfilling God's plan without ever drawing a breath? What privilege God has given that tiny one! He or she never had to strive to be an important part of the Kingdom of God. There was never a time that your child had to make the choice to follow God or turn away. Just the mere fact that the child existed can bring glory to God! Hard to comprehend? No doubt. But to bring glory to God is the reason we were created in the first place! And God and God alone is the One who knows how to bring glory to Himself through tragedy such as this.

When it feels like God is too late to help you, think of the tomb. Surely, the ones who loved Jesus felt the same. The one you would give your life for has no life to offer. Death is the apparent victor. But hold on! Resurrection day is coming! The grave need no longer be a reminder of death, but a reminder of the resurrected life of your baby. Just as Christ used a tomb to proclaim His victory over Death, He can use the death of your baby to reinforce your acceptance of eternal life! Jesus lives! So does your baby! And just as Jesus showed the disciples, eventually may you see how God really is working and moving through this excruciating time, even though you cannot see it with natural eyes or understand with mortal minds.

So many people lose their faith when they lose their baby. Have you? Do you find that you're questioning everything you've ever held true and sacred? If the very foundations of what you believe have been shaken, take my hand and step with me inside an empty tomb.

Mary Magdalene loved Jesus. She couldn't help it. He had rescued her from so much. She just couldn't stay away from the tomb. When she was tormented by a multitude of demons, Jesus stepped in and cast them away. They were no longer permitted to make her heart their home. Mary knew that Jesus had the power to transform her life forever. Every moment of peace and sanity was a gift from Him. Somehow, deep inside, she realized that Jesus' death just couldn't be the end of the story.

The Bible tells us that Mary slipped away to Jesus' tomb while it was still dark outside. When she got there, she saw that the tomb was opened! What happened? All she knew was that she needed help and she ran to the disciples.

The Bible tells us that the disciples thought Mary Magdalene's news was pure nonsense. What do you mean, the stone is rolled away? You really believe Jesus is no longer in the tomb? After all, she was the one who had been out of her mind. Her heart had once been a place of residence for evil. Had the pressure of stress and grief sent her off the deep end once again? They knew what they saw. They heard the crowd. The blood splashed on their shoes. They knew God messed up this time.

They all knew but Peter. Peter—who really did blow it. Peter—who turned his back on Jesus and cursed His Name. Something sparked in Peter that day when he heard what Mary had to say. Luke 24:12 says Peter got up and ran to the tomb. I can just see his fishing gear bouncing across the room as he jumped to his feet and headed out the door! Isn't that just like Peter? He can't do anything half-way. He didn't just *go* to the tomb. He *ran!* He didn't just stop by on his way home. He stopped what he was doing and ran to the tomb so that he could see for himself that Jesus really was who He said He was. One look at an empty tomb and Peter walked away confused and marveling at what had happened. He had seen blinded eyes opened, watched as thousands were fed with only a few morsels, walked on the water with Jesus. But one look inside an empty cave sent Peter stumbling home with his mouth hanging open!

Mary Magdalene couldn't be satisfied to just see an empty tomb. She had to see *Jesus*! When your heart hurts, do what Mary Magdalene did that day. Look for Jesus. The one who redeems. The One who heals. The One who knows the hurt inside knows how to bring peace to one who has once lived in a place of torment. Look for Jesus!

Can you imagine what Mary Magdalene must have thought when she laid eyes on Jesus? We know that she didn't recognize Him at first, because in John 20, the Bible tells us that she thought

He was a gardener. In despair, she began telling this kind man that if He would just tell her where His body was, she would take care of everything. But then He called her name! Everything changed when Jesus, the One she had loved and lost, called her by name.

Imagine for one moment what it will be like when you finally hear your child call you by name. "Mama." "Daddy." You won't be standing at a graveside as Mary Magdalene was that day. No, you'll be standing on streets of purest gold! But just as it was for Mary Magdalene, your life will never be the same!

Can't you hear Mary as she runs to tell the disciples she had seen Jesus alive again? "I've seen Him! I've seen the Lord! What are you just standing there for? Don't you believe me?" Wild-eyed Mary running breathlessly through the door telling them the very thing they most want to hear, but can't force themselves to believe! Jesus has conquered Death and *He is alive!*

Friend, if your faith has been shaken, and you just don't know what to believe, won't you take the example of Peter and run with it? Run to Jesus. He hasn't failed you even if the circumstances surrounding your life are demanding that He has. Or perhaps you're more like Mary Magdalene. Your heart is broken, but you just can't stay away from Jesus. You've got to see Jesus! Something deep inside of you still believes in His promises. Just as He never messed up when the Hebrews boys were thrown into a fiery furnace, just as He arrived right on time when Lazarus died, and just like He completed God's purpose as He hung on Calvary's tree, He is still in control of your life, your family and your future. The death of your baby has not crippled Him. The loss of your child did not knock Him off His throne. God and God alone knows just how to turn this tragedy into triumph and turn your mourning into dancing. Seem impossible? So did Calvary. God used the most horrific event in mankind's history to provide a way to reconcile us again. Imagine what He can accomplish in your life!

Learning from David

⌘

David is such an amazing Biblical character. We find him in fields with sheep and in battlefields with giants. He's been a shepherd and a king, a poet and a songwriter, a faithful husband and an adulterer. We see him charging into battle and hiding in caves. We also find him huddled in grief over the lifeless body of his son. In many ways, David was no different from you and me. Although he was a mighty king, David had to live through the same mind-numbing pain you find yourself in. David's baby died and he was powerless to stop it.

The story of David is a beautiful illustration of life continuing after heartache. Although he was a parent grieving the death of his child, the Bible never says that was useless after his loss. Nor does it say that his life was without joy. How did David survive and how did he continue to thrive?

David found the answer to surviving grief. First of all, he knew what weapons to take with him into war. He took only certain weapons into battle, and left ordinary firearms alone. He knew just which armor to employ and he knew which armor to lay down. Secondly, this former shepherd boy knew that his Good Shepherd would watch out for him. He felt the comfort of His rod and His staff leading him through the darkest valley he'd ever traveled.

Why not sit at the feet of this shepherd boy turned king and learn from his experience? Like you, he had to stare death in the face and choose whether to worship through his tears. Yet trusting in the

Good Shepherd gave him the strength he needed to walk through the valley of the shadow of death.

Well friend, I have an invitation for you.

Stroll down to the creek with me. Dip your toes in the stream.

There are stones to gather and giants to slay.

Weapons of Your Warfare

Then David said to the Philistine, "You come to me with a sword,
a spear, and a javelin, but I come to you in the name of the LORD
of hosts, the God of the armies of Israel, whom you have taunted.
This day the LORD will deliver you up into my hands,
and I will strike you down and remove your head from you.
And I will give the dead bodies of the army of the Philistines this
day to the birds of the sky and the wild beasts of the earth,
that all the earth may know that there is a God in Israel, and that
all this assembly may know that the LORD does not deliver
by sword or by spear; for the battle is the LORD's
and He will give you into our hands."
I Samuel 17:45-47

Everybody loves the story of David and Goliath. The power of the underdog! No one would ever debate the fact that it was impossible for David to defeat Goliath. Goliath was nine feet tall—David was a kid. Goliath was protected to the teeth with impenetrable metal armor. David had a few rocks in his pocket. Goliath had taunted and tortured armies for decades. David had taken care of sheep. No, Goliath was much too big an enemy for David to have a chance at all. Too intimidating. Too mean. Too powerful for everyone else to face. Too bad nobody told Goliath that David was coming against him in the Name of God!

David and King Saul had a history together and David had found favor in his sight. Saul knew Goliath would be prepared and he wanted to make sure that David was protected as well. The king brought out his own garments to clothe David, including his armor and bronze helmet. I think the scenario described in Scripture here is just funny! 1 Samuel 17: 39 says that when David put the armor on and tried to pick up the sword that it was so overwhelming that he couldn't even walk! It was too heavy or too big, and David just couldn't handle it! I envision this good-looking kid standing there with the helmet falling down over his eyes and when he tries to push it out of the way so he can see where to go, he trips over the armor dragging the ground, and has to be helped up. This is the valiant warrior who will defeat the champion of Gath? Unsurprisingly, David graciously declined the use of King Saul's armor.

But wait! Isn't armor supposed to protect us in battle? The fight you are waging since your miscarriage is hard! You've been wounded more deeply than you ever dreamed imaginable and you need something to protect you from getting hurt again. It wasn't that armor was a bad thing for David. It's just that he was wearing the wrong armor. It simply didn't fit.

What "armor" have you employed in your war? So many hurting people turn to inappropriate armor to help them through their battle. You place a helmet of alcohol or other mood-altering substances over your mind. At first, it seems to help. It dulls the pain, at least momentarily, and for a while you don't have to think about the miscarriage. You may find it hard to be around people who think you should join life again, so before long you find yourself not wanting to be around anyone. Isolation becomes the breastplate you wear to protect your heart. Many people say they cannot let the tears flow because once they start they fear they'll never stop. Stuffed feelings become your shield to deflect the arrows of hurt and loss of control. Maybe the scariest battle gear is donned when Satan convinces you that God doesn't really love you—or your baby—or He would have protected your pregnancy. Shutting God out can become an almost impenetrable piece of armor.

Think it through: is this armor working? David could have insisted on wearing Saul's armor. True, it may have protected him from Goliath's spear or his javelin but what good would it have done if David couldn't even move while wearing it? Some armor may look like a good idea at the time, but it can become as burdensome as King Saul's was to David. It actually would have been his downfall and Goliath would have been victorious. Why not do as David did? Shed that armor and put your trust totally in God.

Might I make a suggestion to you, friend? You'll find a description of the armor you need many pages and many centuries after David's confrontation with Goliath. Flip over to the book of Ephesians, chapter 6. Verse 13 says, *"Therefore, take up the full armor of God, so that you will be able to resist in the evil day, and having done everything, to stand firm."* Goliath stood firm in his threats against Israel. He had no doubts that he would succeed. He taunted and laughed and tortured, and he stood firm. Do you realize that Goliath never realized that he was no match for God? No giant is big enough to threaten God! Not Goliath and not your giants! None can stand against Him! God is telling you here to put on *His* armor when you face the fight of your life! Gird yourself with the armor He gives you and stand firm!

Without sword or shield, David began to prepare for battle. If this had been in today's world, he may have gathered the most technologically advanced weapons available to him, but we all know the story. David went to a nearby brook and picked up five stones. Nothing more and nothing less. God must love to do things in ways that make no sense! No one would have ever dreamed of going against a man nine feet tall with nothing more than five stones! To be honest, no one should have dreamed of defeating Goliath with five stones. After all, David only used one!

If you could sit down with David right now, share a cup of coffee and ask him about his choice of weapons that day, I'll guarantee you that a slingshot wouldn't even come up in the conversation. He'd never even mention those stones either. Wait a minute! It says right there in black and white in 1 Samuel 17:40 that David, with his sling in his hand approached the Philistine. True. He had his slingshot with him and we know he gathered five smooth stones from a brook. No debate about that. But contrary to what you may have heard in Sunday school all your life, a slingshot full of stones was not the weapon David used to defeat his monstrous enemy that day. The truth, my friend, lies right where your answer lies. Go back and re-read 1 Samuel 17:45:

> *"You come to me with a sword, a spear, and a javelin,*
> *but I come to you in the name of the LORD of hosts,*
> *the God of the armies of Israel, who you have taunted."*

Goliath may have snickered at David. He may have even thrown his head back and laughed. Oh, but the laughing stopped when he ultimately realized the weapon David used against him! He approached this battle between the forces of life and death with the greatest weapon he could ever have at his disposal—the Name of the Lord of hosts!

How fierce is your battle? Are the sounds of the enemy as deafening as the sounds of silence coming from your nursery? Just as David did when he faced the fight for his life, come against the giants in your way with the powerful Name of the Lord! Realize, just as David did, that the battle truly is the Lord's anyway! And just as David did that day in the valley of Elah, you'll find that your giants, no matter how huge and ferocious, can never stand and will fall prey to the Name of the Lord!

Have you ever *really* thought about the Name of God? He has several names and He selected each one for a very specific purpose. He calls Himself by the Names of His choosing so that you can know what you can expect of Him. They are one way He reveals to us just who He is. Because He calls Himself Jehovah Jireh—meaning God our Provider—we can rest assured that He will provide for our needs. Because He calls Himself Jehovah Rophe—God our Healer—we know He heals us. So what weapons—what Names of God—do you need in your arsenal?

To answer that let's think about your giants. David's giant is obvious. His giant was the very thing that those around him feared, the very one who threatened to defeat him that day. The very one that he had no chance of conquering. The conquest of his giant was also the very thing that made David's life a shining example of God's glory!

So what are your giants? Oh, they are there, and there are probably many! Perhaps this is not your first experience on the battlefield of pregnancy loss. Or your second. Or your third. You're a seasoned warrior in a battle you never intended to fight. You've done all you know to do to ensure success this time. But time after time, your giant stands in the way and grasps victory from your hands. Even if you've survived longer and longer each time, it's never been long enough for your baby to survive. Do you tremble at the thought of trying to conceive again because you simply don't think you can survive another miscarriage? The giant of Fear is threatening to destroy you. Come against the giant of Fear in the Name of the Lord! Isaiah 9:6 is your armory, where your weapon can be found! And His Name will be called...*Prince of Peace.* "I come against the giant of Fear in the Name of the Prince of Peace!"

Have friends and family become so uncomfortable by your tears that they have simply stopped coming around or stopped mentioning the baby all together? Are the giants of Loneliness and Isolation tormenting you and screaming out your name so loudly that you have begun to turn away from those you love? Come against the giants of Loneliness and Isolation with the Name of the Friend who sticks closer than a brother (Proverbs 18:24). Are you collapsing at the feet of the giant called Weakness? Don't feel like you're strong enough to last for the duration of the conflict? Defeat the giant called Weakness with the Name of the Lord found in Isaiah 26:4! You'll see the giant of Weakness bow its knee to the Lord Jehovah, our Everlasting Strength!

But wait! There's a giant that seems to scream more loudly and threateningly than all the rest. What about the mighty giant of Sorrow? It's probably the largest and most powerful giant on the battlefield of miscarriage. It has defeated you time after time after time. No weapon you've brandished against it has accomplished much. Time after time, Sorrow comes against you. Time after time, you dissolve into a pile of tears and pain. Since the loss of your baby your heart has been blindsided with pain you never saw coming. Is there a standard to raise against this powerful warrior?

Take heart, hurting friend. Reach back into your quiver and pull out a mighty weapon! It's found in Psalm 3:1-3:

"O LORD, how my adversaries have increased! Many are rising up against me. Many are saying of my soul, 'There is no deliverance for him in God,' But You, O LORD, are a shield about me, My glory, and the One who lifts my head."

Here, the same David who fought with Goliath is calling out to God at another point of conflict in his life. He's telling God how his adversaries have increased and how so many are rising up against him that people are saying there is no help for him. Sound familiar? "I don't guess they'll ever get over losing that baby!" The giant of Sorrow takes another step toward you. "The pain is so deep! The sadness is so profound! I'll never be truly happy again!" Sorrow throws its head back and laughs at your pain!

But just as David did in the valley of Elah, and just as he does here, join all the righteous warriors of the centuries and proclaim to the giant of Sorrow that God is a shield about you! Any fiery darts are forever extinguished when God Himself is your Shield! You may just hear Sorrow begin to take a step back! That's not all! Is your head bowed down with despair and you can hardly lift your face to carry on with your day? Verse 3 says He is your glory and the Lifter of your Head! Come against the giant of Sorrow with the Name of God Almighty, your Shield! God Almighty, your Glory! God Almighty, the Lifter of your Head! The thundering you hear is the giant of Sorrow falling at your feet for all the armies of the world to see!

Take some time and find the Names of the Lord you are given in Scripture. You'll find your answer in His Name! Digging it out for yourself will be one of the most rewarding experiences you could ever hope for. Remember, He promises you'll find what you need. Why not begin your search in Jeremiah 29:13: *"You will seek Me and find Me when you search for Me with all your heart."* You'll find Him to be everything you need Him to be to help you conquer the giants in the battlefield of miscarriage. Do you fear the weapons of your enemies? Fight back with the promise found in Isaiah 54:17, where you are assured that no weapon formed against you will prosper! When you have found verses and Names of the Lord to use in your warfare, remind your enemy that the Word of God will always accomplish what God says it will accomplish (Isaiah 55:11)! You are assured victory through His Word!

Here are some ideas to get you started on your search for the Names of the Lord:

Giants of Negative Thoughts	He's worthy to be praised (Psalm 18:3)
Giants of Misunderstanding	He's the Man of Sorrow, Acquainted with Grief. (Isaiah 53:3) He knows what it feels like to hurt.
Giant of Depression	He's a Wonderful Counselor (Isaiah 9:6). Tell Him all about it.
Giants of Abandonment by family/friends	He's an Everlasting Father (Isaiah 9:6). He'll never leave.
Feeling attacked by your giants	He's the Strong Tower where the righteous run and are safe. (Proverbs 18:10
Don't know what to say to your giants?	He's the Living Word (John 1:1)

Make these truths a reality in your life and not just a principle! Use the Name of the Lord to conquer your giants and your victory is assured! Remind yourself of these truths every day. Say it aloud or write it on note cards to keep in your wallet. Commit them to memory. Write these precious promises down and tape them to your mirror where you brush your teeth so that you see them every day. Do whatever you are most comfortable with to keep the Word of God in front of you all the time. Before long, an amazing thing will happen. You will start to see your giants falling, and you may just find that they are falling *forward.*

When we dream of our futures, none of us envisions heartache and sorrow. No one stares dreamy-eyed into the decades ahead thrilling at the thought of pain. For whatever reason, God has allowed you and your spouse to walk through an intensely painful season. Have you been disappointed with God? It's hard to believe that a God who loves you would sit with arms folded and simply allow your baby to die. I have a profound thought for you: Goliath fell forward.

That's right. Goliath fell forward. Isn't that fabulous? Go back and read verse 1 Samuel 17:49 again: "*...And the stone sank into his forehead, so that he fell on his face to the ground.*" Goliath fell forward! If you are struggling with the idea that God has chosen not to move in the way you've prayed He would, remember that Goliath fell forward.

Ever wonder what God is doing? So many times God just doesn't work like we think He will. How many times have you heard or said "God wouldn't let *my* baby die. He wouldn't give me such a strong desire to have a baby only to let it die in my womb. He's simply not that cruel." You have truly believed deep in your soul that if God really is love like He says He is, He'd never take your baby from your womb before he or she ever got to experience the fullness of life. What happened to your faith when God simply didn't move the way you truly believed He would?

Perhaps your giant is falling forward.

Enabled by the power of God, David's slingshot flung a small round stone hurtling through the air straight to Goliath's forehead. If you could have seen into the spiritual realm that day, I believe you would have seen a very holy hand reach down and guide that tiny stone to the exact spot where it needed to land on Goliath's head to defeat the enemy of the armies of Israel. I also believe that at the moment of injury, you also would have seen that same hand reach down and knock Goliath flat on his ugly and thoroughly confused face!

Why did God do this? Don't you know that every on-looker on that battlefield must have scratched his head that day? Picture it. A nine-foot tall giant. A little kid with a slingshot. Whose morbid sense of humor sent that kid out there? Harder to believe than the choice of opponents was the apparent choice of weapon. A slingshot? Did this kid really understand his foe? He's not trying to knock a pomegranate out of a tree! It's not even a lion or a bear! This guy is the champion of the armies of Gath! He's no battle-virgin! Goliath has killed more men than that kid even knows, and he's coming with a slingshot?

Listen to the sounds of battle! Goliath laughing, the shwoop, shwoop of the slingshot, the fwoop of the stone sailing through the air, the stone hitting the forehead with the sound more like a boulder falling off a cliff than a pebble making contact with a giant's brow! All of a sudden, there's a cessation of the deep, husky, demonic laughter that's suddenly replaced with a guttural groan! The air is filled with the sharp sound of Goliath catching his last breath, his eyes widening and then rolling back, closing for the last time. The armies stand breathless as they watch Goliath teetering forward, back and then time standing still as he falls forward with a gigantic thud, ground shaking, dust billowing all over the soldiers lining the field, as clouds of dust settle! All they see is their hero dead and disgraced, face down in a pool of his own blood!

Now envision this scene with me: Everyone else is starting to rejoice. Philistines are running for cover, and David is handing out his holy "I told you so's!" But before David could make his way to Goliath's corpse to make good on his promise of decapitation, surely someone must have noticed how Goliath fell.

I picture a battle-weary soldier standing on the sidelines. He'd watched many a man fall to their death on a battlefield, but none like this. Mouth open and steps growing faster and faster, he creeps up closer to the giant dead man lying just yards ahead. How can this be? *He's lying face down!* He was hit in the *forehead*, not the back of the head! If he was hit in the forehead with enough force to take his life, his head should have snapped back and his unseeing eyes gazed heavenward. There's simply no way he could have fallen on his face! It's just impossible! But some way, some how, Goliath fell forward!

Let's talk again about the death of your baby. You never dreamed you'd hear this phrase. You never thought you'd ever stare the death of your baby in the face. You didn't choose this battlefield, but here you are. How could God have possibly asked you to face off with this enemy? You're not capable.

Good news, friend. You're right! You're not capable of defeating this enemy! Just as David was not able of his own accord, neither are you. Here's the best news—God is! When David made his bold proclamation to Goliath that in just moments death would call out his name, he reminded Goliath that the battle is the LORD'S! When Goliath fell forward instead of backward, it had to be by the hand of God. Only God's ability did this. It was humanly impossible for a young kid to defeat a huge and experienced warrior like Goliath with a slingshot and a rock. Only God's ability did this. Everyone on that battlefield that day had to recognize this. They were soldiers and they knew David could not do what he went out there to do. God's ability showed through loud and clear and was made irrefutably evident by a giant falling forward.

Why does this matter? Why did God do this? Because God doesn't always work the way we think He should. When you survive a sorrow as debilitating as the death of your baby, yet you can stand and say God is faithful, your giant falls forward. When you keep going to church and keep worshipping God through your tears, your giant falls forward. Wouldn't it have made more sense for Goliath to fall backward? That was what was supposed to happen. Wouldn't it have made more sense for someone else to lose their baby? Someone who didn't want their baby? Someone who wouldn't have taken care of their baby? Wouldn't it make more sense for *anyone* else to lose their baby rather than you? When you still place your trust in an unseen God who simply did not answer prayer the way you begged Him to, your giant falls forward!

Like it or not, people are watching you as you journey through this season in your life. When others see you stand on the battlefield of grief and proclaim through your tears that even though you don't understand, even though you would never have chosen this path, you still believe and trust in your Savior, your giant falls forward. Maybe you've never trusted Him before but since the death of your baby, you've realized you cannot travel this road alone and you've chosen to take a huge step of faith and place your trust in this unseen

God. What meaning this gives to your baby's short life! Only God can do this. Only God can sustain you through so great a trial as the death of your baby. Only God can make that giant fall forward. Only God can bring you through this valley with more strength and newfound faith. Only God can make that giant fall forward.

A woman once told me that after years of trying to conceive, she finally got a positive pregnancy test. Years of tears and sorrow were replaced in an instant with tears of inexplicable joy as friends and co-workers began celebrating and planning a shower! In a heart-breaking turn of events, a single phone call from a doctor's office shattered her joy. She would never hold this baby she was dreaming of. She was placed right back in the battlefield of sorrow and was forced to pick up her armor and weapons once again.

Here's the part I want you to focus on. The woman's co-workers watched her like a hawk. They wanted to know if the faith she had professed through the years was enough to sustain her through her grief. Guess what. It was! Because of this massive disappointment, she was able to share her faith in a brand new way. As the tears flowed and dripped off her chin, she kept saying that although she didn't understand, she knew God was in control. And her giant fell forward.

God used a confusing situation in her life to showcase His faith-fulness to her. Isn't He a brilliant God? Only God could take sorrow so profound and bring beauty from it. Only God can use hurt to show you His comfort and healing. Only God's ability can make your giant fall forward.

Soldiers line your battlefield. Some have fought the same fight as you. Others are blissfully unaware that their names will soon be called to join the same battle. Many run in terror when the subject of miscarried babies is even mentioned. But all are watching. You have a great opportunity to let God use this trial and turn it for good. Just as David impossibly conquered Goliath through the Name of the Lord, you can impossibly conquer your own giants the same way. After all, remember that the battle is not yours anyway. It belongs to the Lord. Just as all the people there that day knew God was God and there was no other, imagine the undeniable testimony your life can have when those around you witness your survival. They'll know beyond a shadow of a doubt that God really is who He says He is and that He has fought your battles for you.

Does placing your trust in God and allowing Him to shine through this heartache in your life mean you won't miscarry again? I don't know. Will you eventually bring home a healthy baby? Only heaven knows. Here's what I do know. Wrap yourself in truth, your heart protected by righteousness, a shield of faith to extinguish the fiery darts of your enemy, and cover your mind in the Salvation that comes from a true relationship with Jesus Christ. Then fight your battles with the sword of the Word of God and the Name of God. No enemy can withstand this armor and sword! Just as David did that day, come against your giants—giants of depression, fear, marital discord, anxiety—with the Name of the Lord and the sword of the Word of God! Just as Goliath did that day, you'll see your giants fall forward and crumble at your feet. And just as the armies of the Philistines truly learned that day, those around you will know there really is a God fighting your battles for you! Your life can be a ticker tape parade of God's glory for the soldiers returning from the most devastating battle life has to bring!

Stupid Sheep

I recently read a very interesting story on the internet. Somewhere in Turkey 450 sheep plummeted to their death as one by one they blindly followed each other over a cliff. The only reason there were not more wooly fatalities was simply because the carcasses of the first several hundred sheep cushioned the fall for the remaining 800 or so. Eyewitnesses described a huge pile of dead sheep with hundreds of others literally taking a flying leap off a cliff and landing on the mound of carcasses. Can you imagine such a scene? The villagers were devastated and had no idea how they would survive financially. If it were not so tragic for the sheep farmers, it would be a hilarious story.

What caused this strange scenario? No one forced the sheep. There was no scantily clad, sexily shorn ewe standing at the base of the mountain whistling for the attention of the males on top of the hill. There was nothing apparently appealing about sailing off a cliff other than the thrill of a moment of weightlessness. So what happened?

Nothing happened. That's the whole problem. The shepherds of this flock got hungry and decided to have some breakfast. As they were munching on their Wheaties (or whatever Turkish shepherds eat for breakfast), lambs were literally flying from safety to their demise. As the shepherds filled their stomachs, the sheep landed on theirs. The shepherds were doing nothing to protect the sheep. The shepherds were doing nothing to guide the sheep. The shepherds were doing nothing to show affection or attention to the sheep. As a result, the sheep perished.

Sheep are really dumb animals. They simply cannot survive on their own. They have to have the guidance and protection of a conscientious shepherd. A shepherd who has scouted out the pastures to make sure there are no hazards. A shepherd who is willing to put himself in harm's way to keep his lambs out of danger. These sheep didn't have a good shepherd. We do.

The names ascribed to the Lord in Scripture are not there simply because they sound high and lofty. These names describe His holiness, His ability, and who He is. It is no mistake that He is called the Good Shepherd.

The Good Shepherd lays down His life for His sheep. Rather than leave you for even a moment, your Good Shepherd leads you beside still waters so you don't drown in harsh, fast moving whirlpools of sorrow. He'll stay awake all night and watch over you as you sleep, protecting you from harm. And He'll never leave you to go have breakfast. Instead, He'll prepare a table for when you stand in the presence of your enemies, even if that enemy is the loss of your precious baby.

Perhaps the most beautiful thing your Shepherd does for you is walk with you through the valley of the shadow of death. There are probably no situations we face in life where we need our Shepherd more than our journey through the grief that follows the death of a baby. The path is too steep and rocky to try it alone. The shadows grow bigger and bigger and we're lost in the darkness. We're totally clueless as we try to find which direction to travel. We're just stupid sheep. But we have a brilliant Shepherd!

Psalm 23 is probably one of the most beloved passages of Scripture in the entire Bible. It has been read at millions of funerals, prayed over countless hospital beds and cried at the sides of untold numbers of gravesites. It offers us hope and encouragement in the most difficult situation we will ever experience—the death of someone we love.

Do you realize who God used to write Psalm 23? David. What do you know about David? This is the same little guy who killed not only a bear, but also a lion with his bare hands. The same young man who killed a nine-foot tall giant with only one small little rock he found in a brook. The same man who assumed the throne of Israel and became their beloved king. He was also a distraught father who faced the daunting task of burying his baby.

David experienced the same excruciating loss that you have suffered. Read his story in the book of 1 Samuel for yourself. You may find a lot of similarities between this king and you. King David and his wife have had a baby and they loved him passionately—just like you loved your baby. Although we don't know the specifics of his illness, we are told that the baby became deathly sick. Maybe they knew why, maybe they didn't. All that mattered was that something was terribly wrong. Just as you may have pleaded with an unseen God to restore life to the tiny baby in your womb, you'll see that David too begged God to spare the life of his very ill baby for seven days. Perhaps you've prayed until you simply didn't know what else to pray, as words escaped your heart and sobs took over. In David's story, you'll find that for seven days, David did nothing else but pray. He wouldn't eat. He couldn't sleep. All he did was cry out to God pleading with Him to save his baby. Keep on reading and you'll discover that like your story and much to the devastation of David's heart, God chose not to heal David's son, and the baby slipped away into eternity.

Before the loss of your baby, you probably never would have realized how one little person so tiny could possibly create a wound in your heart so great and so overwhelming that you feel you may never recover. How could one so small, perhaps even unseen by human eye and to the world so insignificant become the total focus of your life, your thoughts, and your emotions? Friend, you have an understanding brother in King David. Just as you have been torn apart by your loss, David's heart was ripped in two as well. The gallons of tears you've cried could match his own. Before time began, God knew you would feel totally misunderstood as you traveled through the valley of grief and loss, so He included the story of David in His never-changing, life-giving Word. Let's sit at the feet of this healed sufferer and glean from his experience.

Although you have probably read Psalm 23 hundreds of times and could most likely recite it from memory, as you think about David's situation, re-read this familiar passage of Scripture:

¹The LORD is my shepherd,
I shall not want.
²He makes me lie down in green pastures;
He leads me beside quiet waters.
³He restores my soul;
He guides me in the paths of righteousness
For His name's sake.
⁴Even though I walk through the valley of the shadow of death
I fear no evil, for You are with me;
Your rod and Your staff, they comfort me.
⁵You prepare a table before me in the presence of my enemies;
You have anointed my head with oil;
My cup overflows.
⁶Surely goodness and lovingkindness will follow me
all the days of my life,
And I will dwell in the house of the LORD forever.
Psalm 23

The same David who has wept as he has buried his baby is saying the Lord is his shepherd. The same man who most assuredly felt as if he were going to drown in his own tears is saying that God comforts him. David knew shepherding—he was a shepherd himself! When a lamb would get injured, a shepherd would pour oil into the wound to ease the suffering and promote healing. Here David says that God anoints his head with oil. Just as surely as David knew the pain of loss, He knew the comfort of healing.

Perhaps the most striking portion of this passage is wrapped up in two little words. They really pack a powerful punch! You've probably read them a hundred times and maybe you've gone right past them without realizing what a guidepost they are for someone valiantly trying to navigate the valley of the shadow of death. The first one is nestled right there in the midst of verse 4: *walk.*

Walk? That's the incredibly significant word that will help you survive your grief? I'll bet you thought it was going to be *'restores'* or *'guides'*. Perhaps your heart zoned in on the healing virtue of *"You have anointed my head with oil"*. Isn't it amazing how you can read the same passage of Scripture over and over again throughout the years, yet it still remains fresh and new? Each of us can find specific nuggets of truth to help us while someone right next to us finds something totally different, yet specific to them. For now, let's focus on this commanding little word: *walk*.

Grief is such a terrifying journey when we lose someone we love, and that journey is often misunderstood when the lost treasure is a baby not yet born. Most likely, you've been told—or you will be told—to "get over it". Others may feel you have hurt long enough and it's time to get on to the chore of living once again, but for you it may seem that you are mired down in the swampland of grief and you will never escape. Hurting child, re-read the fourth verse of Psalm 23: Even though I *walk*...

Grief is a journey that must be traveled. The death of your baby is not something that you can get over in a couple of days. You didn't dream of your baby and fall in love with him or her in a couple of days, and you will not recover from this loss in a few days. Maybe that's why David said he had to *walk* through the valley of the shadow of death. It simply takes time. There is no mention of *running* through grief, or hurrying on your way. No, the journey cannot be rushed. Have you noticed that David didn't say *"Yea, though I* crawl *through the valley of the shadow of death..."* Nor does it say, *"As I* sat there..." David said that he had to *walk* through this valley.

There are certain milestones that you must face following your miscarriage. There will be days when sorrow tightens its grip on your heart and you wonder if you'll survive. You're simply walking through the valley. When your due date approaches and sorrow reminds you that you should have had a baby today, keep walking. Anniversaries of your loss will be difficult as will the inevitable showers or baby dedications you'll have to face. But just as David did, keep walking and eventually these excruciating landmarks on the backdrop of grief will be behind you.

As you walk, there's good news for you, friend! It's found in the second power-packed word I want you to think about in this Psalm. When David told us that he *walked* through his grief, realize that he also said he walked *through* the valley!

You cannot avoid the grief. You must go *through* it. We cannot go around it, under it or over it. We very simply must journey *through* it. There's no getting by it and no avoiding it, so give yourself the luxury of grieving this loss. I realize it sounds crazy to call grieving a luxury, but you will do yourself a favor if you will not try to stuff your emotions and deny yourself the grief that a mother or father feels when their baby dies. If you need to cry, don't hold back. There is no shortage of tissues. If you need to talk about your baby, talk about your baby, even if you are your own audience. Sharing with others who have experienced the same sorrow can be such a healing experience. If you can't find a support group, why not start your own? God has trusted you with the most intense emotion a human being can experience. You may not have ever thought you'd be strong enough to survive such a trial, but God knew you could. He will not tempt you beyond what you can bear, so grieve to fullest extent of your emotions. David walked through his grief and eventually he got to the other side. Good news, friend. When you keep walking, you'll get *through* your valley too!

"But I can't keep going. I'm stuck!" Maybe this is the cry of your broken heart. It may be tempting to pull the covers over your head and hide from life for a while as you doubt that you really can walk through this valley. It hurts to lose a baby you've wanted so badly only to see constant reminders of your loss in every pregnant belly and every infant car seat that seem to throw themselves in your path. Grieve your loss, but don't get stuck there. God promises you life more abundantly (John 10:10) and that means you don't have to get stuck in grief and stay there from now on. The very fact that God has a great plan for you is proof that He didn't intend for you to get stuck in your grief and that your life still has meaning and purpose even after a miscarriage!

Have you ever been to the beach? I must say that I think the oceans with their sandy frames have to be some of God's most magnificent of all His earthly creations. He was really having a good day the day He made them! The next time you go to the beach, I have an assignment for you. Walk along the water's edge where the water just laps up on your feet, no higher than your ankles. Take your time and look out over the waves, feel the cool splash of water on your toes and marvel as God blows His breeze through your hair. After you've enjoyed creation for a few moments, face the waters and just stop walking. Let the waves splash over your feet again and again. Don't take a step. Don't wiggle your toes. Just stand there. Pretty soon, you'll notice something. Your feet have disappeared! The longer you stand, the deeper your feet are being buried in the sand until you find it's getting a little hard to keep your balance. Little by little, the sandy water swirls around you and little by little, you find yourself getting stuck. It doesn't take a brilliant scientist to tell you why you're stuck: you've stopped walking.

Walking through to the other side of sorrow is a tall order, but the valley is not the place you want to stay longer than you have to. But how is it possible to keep walking when the burden of pain is so great? Grieving is hard work, but God knows you can walk through this valley whether you realize you can or not. Need proof? The answer is found only a phrase away: "I will fear no evil, *for You are with me...*" He knows you can walk through the valley, because He's walking the journey with you.

God is walking with you through this valley in your life! He's not leaving you alone to figure out what to do. God is walking with you. Not running ahead and getting annoyed because it's taking you too long to get through it. He makes you lie down in green pastures. Not lagging behind and not caring that you don't know what to do next. He's leading you and guiding you in the right paths. God is walking *with* you. Step by step. Tear by tear. He was there with you in the doctor's office that day. He was with you as the awful realizations began to sink in. He was with you when you had to tell family and friends that you wouldn't be bringing home a baby. He's with you as your tears flow. He's with you in those precious, rare moments when you forget you have a problem. He's with you through the nights when sleep escapes you. He's walking with you right now.

And He doesn't come empty handed. God is our Great Shepherd and He carries with Him His rod and His staff. Why does that matter? Because the rod and staff are symbolic of His comfort. He walks with you and He comforts you. Have you felt His comfort? Remember the kind word of a friend who tries to understand your struggle though she's never had to face the valley? You've felt the comfort of the Shepherd's rod. Perhaps your pastor's message somehow reached straight across the pulpit and into your heart. Your Shepherd's staff is leading you through your sorrow. Maybe you've found an uplifting website or an encouraging support group. Perhaps you've felt the wounds in your heart beginning to heal and tears slowly starting to lessen. However comfort comes, it comes from the Great Shepherd Himself.

Perhaps you feel as if you have been grieving far too long, and you're afraid you'll feel like this forever. On the contrary, friend. God promises that this is a *season* in your life, and not your assignment for the remainder of your days. Seasons don't last forever. They last for an appointed time and then a new season takes its place. The same is true for your heartbreak. There is a time to grieve, a time to hurt and a time to weep. But just as there is a season for sorrow, there is a time to lay down the grief and experience a season for healing. Read with me from Ecclesiastes 3 (KJV):

> *¹To every thing there is a season, and a time to every purpose*
> *under the heaven:*
> *²A time to be born, and a time to die; a time to plant,*
> *and a time to pluck up that which is planted;*
> *³A time to kill, and a time to heal; a time to break down,*
> *and a time to build up;*
> *⁴A time to weep, and a time to laugh; a time to mourn,*
> *and a time to dance;*

Laughing takes the place of weeping, mourning gives way to dancing and eventually sorrow bows down to joy.

2 Corinthians 1:3 says that God is the God of all comforts. He knows just what you need and just when you need it. Eventually, you'll find that the grip of sorrow has begun to lose its grip on your heart. The situations that used to devastate you now only make you somewhat uncomfortable. Your season of healing is coming. Rather

than weeping, you'll find that you're sleeping through the night. Your season of healing is coming. And one wonderful day you'll be able to think about your baby and envision your reunion in heaven rather than your separation on earth. Your season of healing is coming.

Is it difficult for you to imagine not grieving anymore? Grief has become so much a part of your life since your miscarriage, it may seem that grief defines who you are. You do not leave the memory of your baby in the valley of the shadow of death simply because you complete the grieving process. Don't allow Satan to convince you that allowing yourself to heal means you don't treasure your child or that you are in some way betraying the memory of your baby or the place that he or she holds in your life. This experience, devastating though it is, is a part of your history. It's a part of what makes you who you are, but it does not have to define you. To cease to grieve doesn't mean that you'll never remember this season in your life; it just means that it isn't the main focus of your life anymore.

There is a very important gadget in your automobile without which you should never attempt to drive. It's your rearview mirror. You need it to drive safely around your town, no matter if you live in a huge, bustling metropolis or if you live in Po-dunk Holler. However, what would happen if you drove everywhere looking only in your rearview mirror? Can you imagine never looking through your windshield, but keeping your eyes fixed on that one spot to see what is behind you? What would happen? Before long you'd have an accident! You may hit another car, or slam into a tree. You may even be totally lost and not be able to find the way to your destination. Most likely you'd get hurt and others may as well. There is a 100% guarantee that you simply cannot drive while always looking behind you.

Do you realize that your life is the same way? You cannot always remain in your grief, looking back at the sorrow of loss. You'll find that you become lost and cannot get to the destination God has for you. You'll be hurt, and most likely others will be hurt as well. God never intended for you to go through life looking behind you.

That's not to say that you don't remember your baby or this difficult time in your life. Every time you drive your car, you glance in your rearview mirror, but your eyes don't stay fixed there. Glancing in the mirror shows you where you've come and what's behind you. Maybe you look there and you see rough roads that you've come safely through. However, eventually you have to look ahead. When your healing has come to your heart, glance back every once in a while. See the rough roads that your Shepherd has led you safely through. You may see others there who need to know that they can survive the same journey you've taken. Then shift your eyes forward and trust the Shepherd to lead you to new pastures.

There's a final similarity between David's life and yours, even if this scene has not played out on the stage of your life yet. David's life didn't end when his baby died and yours doesn't have to either. Not by a long shot! David grieved his loss and kept serving God even though God didn't move in the way he prayed He would. What would have happened if David had given up and believed Satan's lie that it's impossible for life to be good and productive after the death of a baby? He would have lived a life of sorrow and despair. We may never have had the 23rd Psalm and countless millions of people would never have gleaned comfort from those words. David trusted in God and kept walking. Friend, God loves you as much as He loved David. He stands ready to be your Shepherd and guide you through the valley of the shadow of death. He is your Good Shepherd and He doesn't come empty handed. He brings with Him His rod and staff—His comfort for your hurting heart. He'll give you goodness and mercy to surround you for the entirety of your life. If you keep walking through your sorrow, eventually you'll come *through* the valley of sorrow and find life to be fulfilling again.

He leads…
He guides…
He comforts…
He walks with you through the valley of the shadow of death.

Mary's Oil
An Unrecoverable Sacrifice

³Then Mary took about a pint of pure nard, an expensive perfume; she poured it on Jesus' feet and wiped his feet with her hair. And the house was filled with the fragrance of the perfume. ⁴But one of his disciples, Judas Iscariot, who was later to betray him, objected, ⁵"Why wasn't this perfume sold and the money given to the poor? It was worth a year's wages." ⁶He did not say this because he cared about the poor but because he was a thief; as keeper of the money bag, he used to help himself to what was put into it.⁷ "Leave her alone," Jesus replied. "It was intended that she should save this perfume for the day of my burial.
John 12:3-7

⁸She has done what she could.
Mark 14:8

¹³I tell you the truth, wherever this gospel is preached throughout the world, what she has done will also be told, in memory of her."
Matthew 26:13

The story of Mary pouring her oil at the feet of Jesus is such a beautiful picture of love and devotion. This is the same Mary who wept at Lazarus' tomb, the same sweet Mary who wept in the presence of the disciples one day as she took such a chance and such a treasure and poured oil on Jesus' feet. It seems that for Mary, kneeling at the feet of Jesus was perhaps her favorite place to be. It's where she went in sorrow. It's where she went in worship. The same feet where she crumbled when she was so overcome with grief is where she now bows in humble adoration, giving Him the absolute best she can offer Him. Her tears of sorrow falling like rain and running down the side of His dusty, calloused feet have been replaced with tears of gratitude and oil of anointing. Go with me to John 12 and let's visit Mary as she once again falls at the feet of this blessed Savior.

Jesus had come to what must have been one of His favorite places. He was once again visiting Mary, Martha and Lazarus at the home of Simon the leper. Jesus had already raised Lazarus from the dead, and now, six days before the Passover, Jesus and His disciples joined the siblings for a meal.

As was typical for these folks, Martha was busy scurrying around, making sure that this dish was cooked properly, that everyone had enough to eat, and of course, there was plenty to clean up after serving all those messy disciples! Suddenly, the atmosphere and the noise levels in the room shift. Mary is quietly and reverently slipping up to the table where Jesus and Lazarus are reclining and enjoying food and fellowship. Can't you see her? A beautifully intent look in those dark, almond shaped eyes. Her gaze so fixed on Jesus that I wonder if she even heard the murmuring going on around her.

Mary comes, not carrying food for the meal, but a beautiful alabaster treasure box. The room grows so still that the only sound anyone hears is the sound of Mary's tears cascading down her olive face and dripping on the dusty floor as she bends to kneel in front of Jesus. What is she doing? Is she going to embarrass her family in front of her guests?

As the crowd around her watched with great annoyance, Mary began her show of devotion to the One she loved more deeply than any other. Mary's act of devotion was not accepted by those surrounding the Lord. Realize that Mary was described in Luke 7 as "a woman in the city who was a sinner", and this story took place in the home of a religious leader. Those in attendance did not approve of Mary or her actions. The people knew her history, but Jesus knew her heart.

Have you ever wondered what was going through Mary's mind when she humbly yet boldly proclaimed her love for Love Himself? Paying no attention to those who simply did not understand, Mary took this fine alabaster vessel, crushed it and poured the costly, precious treasure on the feet of her Lord.

We know that this was the most expensive and rare ointment that she could have possibly gotten her hands on. Not something that she could have gone into the marketplace to purchase. Most likely, it was something she was never able to replace. No, this was a greater treasure. Something precious. Something she had no doubt guarded with her life. Yet here we see that in the greatest act of love she could have performed for her master, Mary pours the oil on the feet of Jesus. And just as Mary voluntarily poured out her oil on Him as a sacrifice of love, in only a short time, Jesus would so pour out His blood for her.

The significance of what Mary did that day is startling. When someone died in Biblical times, their body was anointed with oil in preparation for burial. Somehow, Mary knew Jesus was facing death. What she did when she poured her most precious treasure on Him was her way of preparing His body for death. Jesus acknowledged this and even tried to explain this to His disciples.

Tears cascading down her face, Mary rubs her oil on Jesus' calloused feet. Wouldn't you love to have been able to hear what she must have been saying to Him? And the smell! The sweet smell of spikenard mingled with the fragrance of a pure love offering filled the room where the company had gathered. As was customary in that day, when she was finished anointing His feet, Mary swept her long, dark hair from behind her back and began to dry His feet. Her hair must have soaked up much of the fragrant oil. Don't you imagine that for days every time she turned her head she would smell the aroma and remember the love she had for her Savior and the love He had for her? What love her heart now held when only a short time before, it had been swaddled in grief!

Perhaps you have found yourself preparing for the death of your baby. The doctors say it's inevitable. Your heart and mind say it's incomprehensible. Yet you have that horrible knowledge that death is coming. Hormone tests and blood levels are not usually wrong. Barring a miracle, death will visit your home and your womb. The embrace of sorrow grows ever tighter.

If so, have a seat on that dusty floor by Mary. She would understand your heart breaking in two as you ask every question, pray every prayer. She understood, much as you may have, that death was coming.

Surely Jesus' body looked healthy enough. There is no mention of the disciples asking for a physician. They wouldn't have had to look far—Luke was a physician! Apparently Luke was there, because he gives an account of the story in the book of Luke chapter 7. Surely, if Jesus had looked weak or ill, Dr. Luke would have told Jesus that He needed to lie down. We see nothing of this in any of the four gospels. Jesus had to be physically strong and healthy. He walked everywhere He went and there was no fast food in His day to clog His arteries! Don't forget the events leading up to Calvary. Jesus endured unbelievable physical torture when He was beaten and scourged. This act alone killed many, many men, yet Jesus survived it until the appointed time for Him to lay down His life on the cross. No one else surrounding Jesus caught on to what Mary discovered. Yet somehow, Mary understood that death had an appointment with the Giver of Life, and she felt she had to do something. How interesting it is that she never tried to stop death. She simply helped Jesus to prepare.

Once you make the marvelous discovery that a baby is on the way, you do everything you can to assure that your baby has a healthy environment in which to develop. You take vitamins, you get rest. You forego your favorite soft drinks and chocolate, and replace them with fruits and veggies. Tired? You rest. Hungry? You eat. Men who have never picked up a house-cleaning item in their lives are vacuuming every room and forbidding their glowing wives to touch anything that weighs over a pound and a half. You've never pampered yourself so in your entire life. That's okay! You've never housed such a miracle before!

However, in spite of everything you've done, death somehow takes residence in your womb and your baby slips into eternity. But wait! We'll do another test! Wait! Isn't there a new medicine we can try? Bed rest? You couldn't pull me out of this bed with a team of wild horses! Just tell me what to do—*I'll do whatever I can do to save this baby!*

If sheer determination was enough, if desire was enough, if love was enough, your baby would have lived. You have fought with strength beyond what you were capable of, yet the doctor can only say he's sorry. Every woman who has ever lost a baby to miscarriage is no doubt haunted by the terrifying thought "If only I had done__ _____, my baby wouldn't have died." A woman once tearfully told me that if she had not picked up her suitcase she would never have lost her baby! The suitcase could never have been as heavy as the guilt she carried. Oh, the heartache! Oh, the unfathomable sorrow! Chances are, you did everything you knew to do to have a safe, routine, boring pregnancy, yet somehow it just didn't happen. You did all you could do. Join hands with Mary. She understands.

When Mary displayed her love for Jesus, the disciples began to argue and complain. They were indignant. "Why the waste?" griped Judas, who loved money more than the Master. "Why didn't she sell that stuff? We could've used the money! Why is she pouring it out on the floor?" But before they could grumble and complain too much, Jesus came to Mary's defense. Look at His response. Mary has done what she could. She could not help Jesus avoid His death. She could not take His place in the grave. As much as she would have loved to, she could not run up Calvary's hillside, tear down Jesus' cross, and burn it as firewood. But compassionate, perfect Jesus looks at compassionate, imperfect Mary and her critics in the eye and says "She has done what she could." She poured out her love, she poured out her riches. She knelt at the feet of the One who would conquer death—His own and hers—to prepare Him for the grave. She did all she could do and Jesus called it beautiful. Because of this, Jesus promises that she'll be known throughout time and eternity for doing what she could for someone facing a battle with death.

My friend, won't you hear Jesus saying the same words to you today. "You did what you could." There are so many things you simply cannot do. You cannot force your body to produce the right hormones. You cannot command that every tiny chromosome line up perfectly and divide as they should. You cannot force the tiny heart inside your baby to continue to beat, nor can you erase genetic disorders with a shower of your tears. But you have done what you could. Whether doing what you could involved enduring difficult medical procedures, or even if it was something as unobvious as providing a body in which your baby began to develop, you have done what you could. Perhaps you have stood watch for hours on end beside a tiny incubator and watched as your baby clung to life with the courage of a valiant warrior. Feeling more helpless than you ever could have in all of your life, what did you do? You prayed. You wept. You consulted with doctors and made the best decision you knew how to make. You did your best to let your baby know you were there. You did all you could. And when you have done all that you could, Jesus calls it "beautiful".

She has done what she could.
Mark 14:8

She has done a beautiful thing to me.
Matthew 26:10

Now that you are on the other side of miscarriage or stillbirth, you have a choice to make. What do you do now? Does this great tragedy destroy you? It can, you know. Far too many couples watch the death of their marriage following the death of their baby. No doubt God grieves both losses. Your heart may be crying out—"What other choice is there? My heart died when my baby died! I simply cannot survive this massive loss and grotesque sorrow! I cannot and I do not even want to!"

If this is your heart's cry, you're not alone. An unseen Guest sits with you at every meal, cries every tear you cry, and walks every excruciating step through your journey of grief and loss. God the Father knows first-hand what it feels like to lose a Child to death. *Remember, His Child died too.* Because of this, He can come along side you and carry you when your burden is simply too heavy for mortal shoulders. When your tears fall like raindrops,

His are splashing on the ground right alongside yours. Isaiah 53:3 describes our Lord as a man of sorrows, acquainted with grief. He knows the pain of a heart torn in two by grief, yet He also knows how healing comes.

Even in the darkest, most devastating moments of your life, God has promised to never leave you. Ever. He's there with you through miscarriage. He's there with you through stillbirth. As you stood weeping at a gravesite, He stood closer to you than even your spouse did. As you stared at a stilled sonogram screen, His presence was there even more so than the physician's. He is your Good Shepherd, and He refuses to leave His sheep.

No one, nothing, not even death, is strong enough to tear Him away from your side. Need proof? It's written very plainly in black and white. Look at Romans 8:38:

> *"For I am convinced that neither death nor life,*
> *neither angels nor demons, neither the present nor the future,*
> *nor any powers, neither height nor depth, nor anything else in all*
> *creation, will be able to separate us from the love of God*
> *that is in Christ Jesus our Lord."*

Nothing is strong enough to separate you from the love that God has for you. The powerful, magnetic love that chose to face death itself so that you could stand in the midst of a trial as great as the death of your baby refuses to abandon you for even an instant! Nothing will pull Him away from you—not the death of your baby, not life with all its ups and downs. Not even life without your baby.

When the writer listed all the situations that must bow their knee to the love of God, he listed death first. Why? In the mindset of people in this day, the most important, most powerful person was named first, seated at the first place at the table, given the first position of honor. Maybe he listed death first because he knew that death was the most formidable opponent we would ever face. Tougher than life, tougher than angels or demons, our present or our future. Nothing in all creation can touch us like death, but the writer of Romans wants you to know first that even death is powerless in the presence of God's commanding love for you.

Perhaps you feel like Mary must have felt that day as she poured her most precious treasure on Jesus. That costly oil, kept safely in her beautiful alabaster box. The most costly thing she'd ever held in her hands. We do not read where Mary opened her box and closed it again when she finished anointing Jesus. She could not restore the brokenness of the box. Her alabaster treasure box had to be destroyed in order for her to be able to pour her offering of love on Jesus. This was an all or nothing event. No going back. Things would never again be the way they were.

Out of the brokenness of the alabaster vessel, Mary poured her priceless treasure of love on the One she loved most. The ointment? Costly. Rare. Chances are she was never able to replace it. She could not gather up the oil to reuse at another time. But somehow, she found the courage to pour it out on Jesus. She didn't spill it. There is no record of an accident in this scenario. Just love being poured out of brokenness.

Are you feeling a connection with Mary? "God, here's the absolute best I have to offer. My baby is the greatest treasure I've ever been given. The life of this baby has cost me more than anyone can imagine, and it cannot be replaced." Just as Mary poured her admiration for the Lord out of the brokenness of her vessel, cry out to God from the brokenness of your heart. As Mary poured her oil on Him, pour your sorrow on the feet of the Master. You may just find His tears puddling on the floor with yours.

Just as He did with Mary that day, Jesus will meet your need. In fact, just as He did for her, He'll come to your defense, not turn you away. Unsure? Read Psalm 51:17: *"A broken and contrite heart, O God, you will not despise."* See the word "contrite"? The literal meaning of that word is "crushed" or "mutilated". Bring your crushed and broken heart to the feet of Jesus. Mary's treasure box was crushed and broken before she lavished her treasure on Jesus. Pour your heart out until it runs over Jesus' feet like Mary's oil.

For when you pour the oil of your brokenness on the feet of Jesus, there you'll find your healing. Psalm 34:18 says *"The Lord is close to the brokenhearted and saves those who are crushed in spirit."* Psalm 147:3 says *"He heals the brokenhearted and binds up their wounds."* Need healing for your broken heart? The Lord is close by.

Kneel down at His feet. Do you have wounds that need binding? Pour those hurts out of your broken vessel. He'll apply the healing balm. He knows the cry of your heart even when those around do not understand. He alone knows how to take your mourning and turn it into dancing.

Jeremiah 18 tells us of a potter who was creating a vessel on his wheel. When he looked at the clay vessel, he saw that it was marred. It was wounded. Much like your heart is wounded. But this master potter knew what to do to make the vessel beautiful again. He began to shape and reshape this vessel. If anyone was watching him, surely they thought the vessel would be destroyed and would be worthless to anyone ever again! After all, who could ever use a broken vessel? But the potter doesn't appear to be worried. He knows just what to do. The Bible says he simply remade the vessel, and the vessel became pleasing unto the potter.

Only God knows how to restore brokenness of your heart and make you whole again. You may feel that He's destroyed you with the loss of this baby. Who could ever want or use a broken vessel like you? God. He knows just what to do to create of you a vessel that is pleasing. He remains near to you in your brokenness and knows just how to bind your wounds. The strength of the sorrow that has crushed your heart and your spirit will eventually begin to fade, as the love of the Potter transforms your broken vessel into a new one. An even more beautiful one.

He's working on you.

He's rebuilding.

And He's passionately in love with you enough to do this for you.

They Are Precious in His Sight
Psalm 139

⁷Where can I go from Your Spirit?
Or where can I flee from Your presence?
⁸If I ascend to heaven, You are there;
If I make my bed in Sheol, behold, You are there.
⁹If I take the wings of the dawn,
If I dwell in the remotest part of the sea,
¹⁰Even there Your hand will lead me,
And Your right hand will lay hold of me.
¹¹If I say "Surely the darkness will overwhelm me,
And the light around me will be night,"
¹²Even the darkness is not dark to You,
And the night is as bright as the day.
Darkness and light are alike to You.
¹³For You formed my inward parts;
You wove me in my mother's womb.
¹⁴I will give thanks to You, for I am fearfully
and wonderfully made;
Wonderful are Your works,
And my soul knows it very well.
¹⁵My frame was not hidden from You,
When I was made in secret,
And skillfully wrought in the depths of the earth;

[16]Your eyes have seen my unformed substance;
And in Your book were all written
The days that were ordained for me,
When as yet there was not one of them.
Psalm 139:7-16

The death of a loved one is such a traumatic event, especially when the loss is the unexpected loss of a baby. So many grieving parents torture themselves questioning what the moment of death was like for their child. When the Sago Mine in Upshur County, West Virginia collapsed and the impending death of the miners became certain, one of the men scribbled a note of comfort to his family: "It wasn't bad. I just went to sleep." Knowing that there was an absence of fear and suffering must have brought such comfort to his grieving family.

Perhaps these same thoughts have plagued your heart and mind since the death of your precious tiny one. What happened at the moment of death? What was it like for him or her when they slipped into eternity? I believe the Word of God holds true comfort for your questions.

God was present with your child at the moment of death. You may have been excruciatingly aware that death was coming, or you may not have even known the baby was nestled within your womb, but just as surely as a child lived inside your body, I believe the Creator of the universe took up residence there as well.

You may have never thought about God accompanying your baby in the womb, but He was there. There simply is no place that God is not! Psalm 139 was written by the very same David who, just like you, heavily grieved the death of a precious baby. In His mercy, God pulled back the curtain of understanding and revealed to David that there is absolutely no place where we can go to escape His presence. We cannot go high enough into the heavens to flee His Spirit. He is there! We cannot go to depths low enough to vanish from His view. He is there! Go to the furthest edge of the widest sea. He is there too and His hand is leading His beloved every step of the way. If God is omnipresent—if God really is *everywhere*—then there is no place He is not, and this includes your womb. Why would you think He'd step out at the moment of your baby's death?

Is it hard for you to think of God literally dwelling inside your mortal flesh? He knew it would be, so He wrote it out in black and white for you! Look at the beautiful message we are given in 1 Corinthians 3:16: *"Do you not know that you are a temple of God and that the Spirit of God dwells in you?"* I believe at the last moment of life your baby experienced in your womb, God Himself was there, escorting your baby into eternity. Loving your baby. Leading your baby. Friend, God is active in the womb!

Isaiah 43:1 says *"He who formed you says do not fear. I've called you by name."* Your baby has a name, you know. This may sound strange to you if you lost your baby very early. Maybe you never got to give your child a name. But he or she has one! Your baby's name—even if you never got to name your baby—is written on the palm of God's hand. (Isaiah 49:16)

Oh, how precious your baby is to God! Remember that God *is* love. It's not just that God *loves,* but that God *is* love, and 1 John 4:18 assures you that perfect love casts out fear. At the moment of your loss, whether you knew it or not, God, who is perfect love, was with your baby leading him or her into eternity's hand, and fear had no place. Your baby is someone Jesus shed His blood for. Your baby is someone Jesus prayed for. Your baby is someone Jesus steeled His resolve and went to the cross for.

And your baby is someone Jesus has prepared a place for. Much like you may have prepared a nursery. You anticipated the arrival of a baby. You prepared. You purchased the sweetest things. You washed them so they'd be soft against the delicate baby skin. Yet, somehow, your nursery lies empty. Jesus has prepared in much the same way. Just as you dreamed about your baby, He dreams about you. Just as you purchased the best you could offer, Jesus, too, paid a magnificent price to bring you home. Did you envision your tiny infant sleeping peacefully in the now empty crib? Jesus has envisioned you for centuries strolling down streets of transparent gold. He's waiting for your arrival.

Just as God Himself took His place beside your baby in your womb, Jesus promises to be with us always. You'll find this promise in Matthew 28:20. What blessed assurance! He's with you in the frustrating times when it seems you'll never conceive. He's with you in the joyous time when there are finally two beautiful pink lines on the pregnancy test. He's with you when you feel your baby move and He's with you when you don't. He's with you always. In the good times, in the bad times, in the mundane times and in the excruciating times. He's with you when your heart can hardly fathom the news that your baby has died. He's with you always.

Why does it hurt so badly to lose a baby? Even one only a few weeks post-conception? The answer, my friend, is actually pretty simple. That tiny, little baby—even if he or she was no more than a few cells—was created in the very image and likeness of God Almighty! Oh, the preciousness of this tiny little creature! For a short time, your mortal frame, or that of your spouse, housed the very image and likeness of God Himself. We can only imagine what God looks like. We are told in Scripture that if we were able to look at Him with human eyes that we simply could not take it and we'd fall dead (Exodus 33:20). However, He found a way to give us a glimpse of Himself. He created us in His image and in His likeness. Not exactly like him. He may not have green eyes and brown hair like me, but I've been created in His image and His likeness. Your baby was too, and this makes your baby precious. This is why it hurts so deeply when someone compares your loss to the loss of a pet, no matter how beloved Fido was. An animal simply does not carry the worth that a child carries who has God's fingerprints all over them.

God even says "Before I formed you in your mother's womb, I knew you". He doesn't saunter into a delivery room and look as a newborn takes its first breath and say "Thanks, doc. I'll take it from here!" Birth is not a prerequisite for God's protection, God's love or God's involvement in your baby's life. *Before* your baby was conceived in your body, he or she was already conceived in the heart and mind of God. *Before* you loved your child, God loved your baby. *Before* you prepared your nursery, God had already prepared a place. *Before* you knew you'd lay down your life to save your baby, God laid down His life to save his or her soul. God never planned on waiting until your baby was born to know and love your baby.

It's no wonder that we can proclaim *I am fearfully and wonderfully made!* I can just imagine David when he first got a glimpse of how magnificently he was created. Maybe he looked closely at each finger, examined his outstretched leg and spread his toes! I wonder if he jumped up and ran around, or was this one of those times when he danced until he looked like a madman. *I am fearfully and wonderfully made!* What an incredibly creative God we serve!

In the same manner as David was such a creative success, and just as you yourself are God's most prized masterpiece, your baby was fearfully and wonderfully made. "But my baby's body never got the chance to fully develop. How can you possibly say he or she was fearfully and wonderfully made?" What if abnormalities in the body caused your baby not to survive pregnancy? What then? Blink the tears back long enough to re-read this sacred text and notice what is missing: *I am fearfully and wonderfully made.* It does not say *I am fearfully and wonderfully made as long as I am fully developed with a perfectly functioning body.* Nor does it say *"Because I am fully formed within my mother's womb, I am fearfully and wonderfully made."* The body that housed the precious soul of your baby did not have to be perfect for God to consider it fearfully and wonderfully made or for that tiny body to have invaluable worth. Your baby, no matter how far or how early in its development was fearfully and wonderfully made in the image of God Almighty.

Your baby's life was not a mistake. Your child was not and *is* not unknown to God Almighty, the omnipotent Creator of the universe! God formed your baby Himself. Notice that the verse says *"You formed my inward parts"*. God created this spinning globe that we call home with nothing more than His word, threw the stars into place and caused the sun and moon to take their places in the sky with just an utterance from His lips, yet He knew He wanted more involvement with your child. Just as He formed the oceans and the stars in the sky, He could have spoken the word and life would have begun deep within your body, but He chose to form your baby Himself. Creating, designing and loving your baby with each cell. How precious your child must be to God!

You may have been totally blindsided with the news that you would not take home a healthy baby. The thought of a miscarriage may have been as much of a surprise to you as was the news of your pregnancy, but none of this caught God off guard. Long before your baby was conceived, God knew that your pregnancy would not go as you dreamed. He knew your heart would break and that your mind would question Him. Before you even took a pregnancy test, He knew your faith would be tested. So why did He allow this child to be conceived?

Psalm 139:16 says *"And in Your book were all written the days that were ordained for me when as yet there was not one of them."* God knew every day of your baby's life before you ever experienced the first day of your own. Somehow in God's plan, your baby has achieved all that God laid out for him or her and has done it in a matter of weeks or months! How can a baby born too soon to survive possibly carry out God's plan? Have you searched the Scriptures for answers? Have you pondered what God is doing in your life? Maybe you've found a true relationship with God because you've realized you simply cannot survive this sorrow on your own. Imagine the eternal significance of the life of your baby if his or her presence in your life brings you closer to God! What an awesome honor for your child!

Perhaps you cannot fathom God's plan. It can be hard to see how God is moving when your heart is breaking. Whether or not God chooses to reveal His perfect plan to you this side of eternity, He has never turned away a hurting child—it's simply not in His character. He will lovingly guide you through if you'll allow Him. Hebrews 4:14 reminds you that He understands your hurts and your weaknesses and beckons you to draw near to Him. When grief has weighed so heavily on you, why not fall into the arms of love Himself and tell Him where it hurts. He knows how to comfort you when no one else does.

Don't know where to turn to find help? Look closely at 2 Corinthians 1:3-4. You'll find the God of all comfort who soothes all your hurts. There is no sorrow so great that He cannot reach you and heal your wounds. Are you afraid that you just don't have the strength to walk this road He has chosen for you? I have good news for you, friend. 2 Corinthians 12:9 gently reminds you that His strength is made perfect in your weakness. Do you fear that anxiety has become your master and wraps around you like a garment? 1 Peter 5:7 invites you to cast your anxiety on His broad shoulders because He cares for you. You won't drown in your tears. Wipe them away long enough to read Psalm 56:8. He is aware of each one, has captured them for you, and keeps them in a bottle. "But I just can't survive this sorrow! I don't know how!" Begin by believing the voice of your Savior who tells you that you can do all things through Him (Philippians 4:13).

Do you realize what all these promises of Scripture mean to you? It means you can pour out your heart to God and He'll understand. When friends, family, and even your spouse can't bear to see your tears anymore, God has incredibly broad shoulders for you to cry on and strong arms for you to fall into. Lay your head on His chest and hear His heart beating. A heart that broke just like yours has.

As you find comfort in the bosom of Love Himself, don't forget to look into His eyes and see the promise of a heavenly and eternal reunion with your child. One that will not end in miscarriage. No SIDS allowed inside the gates of pearl! No stilled heartbeats. No blighted ovums. No spontaneous abortions. No grief. No sadness. Just an eternity with the child you've held in your heart so much longer than in your body! And an eternity with a God who loved you enough to orchestrate the death of His only Son to provide a way to reunite you with your child.

There is no doubt that Heaven will be an incredible place that defies the description of man. Never in our wildest imagination could we begin to come close to imagining what God has in store for those who love Him and have received His gift of salvation. Psalm 127 tells us that children are a gift and a reward. If you are a Christian, your gift is unopened, waiting for your arrival in Heaven. What joy your heavenly reunion with your child will bring! Perhaps the only place you ever saw your baby was on a positive pregnancy test or on a stilled sonogram screen. Child of God, you will see your baby one day! You'll see the expressions on their face, smell their fragrance, and hear that precious voice in the place that God has prepared. Was a hospital room the only place you were ever able to hold your stilled child in your arms? One day, because of the sacrifice of Calvary you'll explore together all that Heaven has to offer. For the child of God these are great and precious promises. Not only are you assured an eternity with the baby you have loved and lost, but even more importantly, you will be with the God who loved you enough to sacrifice His baby to allow you an eternity with yours. All you have to do is accept His salvation and with a joyful, redeemed heart join Him at His home. He—and your child—are waiting for you there.

You've suffered one of the greatest sorrows life on earth can bring, and now you must travel the journey of grief. However, you do not have to live in sorrow forever. For the world, death is the end. No reunions. No reconciliation. No hope. Child of God, you don't have to grieve as the world grieves. Unfortunately, Scripture doesn't say "Don't grieve". Wouldn't it be wonderful if God had said "If you are a Christian, you'll never hurt, never feel the sting of pain, and never have to wonder what I'm up to." It sure would make life a lot easier, but how would God really know that we served Him because we loved Him and not because we just wanted a life without problems? No, you must grieve this loss. But here's hope! 1 Thessalonians 4:13 says not to grieve as those who have no hope of a resurrection in Christ Jesus! Grieve as a parent who has the hope of a glorious reunion with your baby in Heaven one day! Your baby didn't cease to exist when you had a miscarriage. Jesus said when He left this planet that He was going away to prepare a place for us—and for your baby. Your baby is very much alive with Jesus Christ in Heaven right now, and as a Christian you can join them one day.

When a baby succumbs to miscarriage, love and sorrow embrace with an intensity you've never known. Two emotions so different meld into each other so that it is almost impossible to tell the difference between the two and each becomes an expression of the other. Their grip is certain and unflinching. They struggle to overcome each other. Love tries to defeat sorrow, sorrow is determined that your love will drown in the flood of your tears and you will succumb to the authority of mourning. You will not feel one without the other. As one emotion's grip weakens momentarily, the other's strengthens.

Eventually, though, love will be the victor in this epic battle for the survival of your heart. Little by little, sorrow begins to let go, and smiles replace the tears. Eventually sorrow loosens its grip and takes a step back. Although the impact of your loss never totally goes away, now it fades into the background and you realize that you really can live again.

Appendix A

Discussion Guide

⌘

The following is offered as a means to help you begin to explore your feelings about what you have read. This discussion guide can be used as part of your own personal devotions or as a catalyst for a dialogue with others who are living an experience similar to your own. 2 Corinthians 1:4 tells us that we will be able to comfort those who are in any affliction with the comfort with which we are comforted by God! In joining with others who are walking the same road, may you find peace and healing for yourself and others. You may want to jot your responses down either on these pages or in a journal and come back to them in the weeks and months ahead. This is a wonderful way to realize just how God is working and moving throughout your story!

The Dance of Love & Sorrow

1. How does your story compare to the dance of Love & Sorrow?

2. Have you begun to hear the music return to your life?

3. Your Father wants "to teach you new songs, songs of hope, songs of joy. Songs that, although muted for a while, did not end when your dance ended." What do you think it will be like when your heart is able to dance again?

A Sleepy Savior

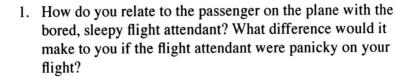

1. How do you relate to the passenger on the plane with the bored, sleepy flight attendant? What difference would it make to you if the flight attendant were panicky on your flight?

2. How have you experienced the physical effects of grief? What do you do to take care of yourself as you grieve?

3. Have you compared yourself to someone you think is grieving more intensely than yourself? Less intensely?

4. Think about Jesus sleeping through the storm. What does it feel like to know that Jesus is simply not worried about your future? How do you feel about Jesus dreaming about you? What do you think He dreamt?

5. How do you relate to the disciples who questioned whether or not Jesus cared if they perished? How does it help you to know that Jesus didn't rebuke the disciples, but He rebuked the winds? Where is your faith?

6. *When* you pass through the water and the rivers... *When* you walk through the fire... How would it be different if this Scripture said "*If* you pass through the water and the rivers...? *If* you walk through the fire...?

7. Perhaps your life is a miracle in the making! Spend some time really thinking this through. Write down what this means to you and save the letter to re-read it one year from now.

8. How do you relate to the butterfly in the hurricane?

Strolling Through Sorrow

1. How can you relate to Peter? To the other disciples?

2. How has your life felt like a tsunami since your miscarriage?

3. Jesus says He prays for you. How does it feel to know He talks to God the Father on your behalf?

4. The waves came upon the disciples in uninterrupted, rapid succession. How have your waves tortured you?

5. Think about Jesus *walking* on the water. Not running, not swimming. How do you think you would have felt if you'd been there that night? How would you have acted? What would you have thought?

6. The disciples had witnessed extraordinary miracles just hours before this incident. Why do you think they doubted Jesus' ability during the storm?

7. Would you have been more like Peter jumping out of the boat or like the other guys staying on board? Why?

8. Think about the storm not dying down even after Peter obeyed Jesus' commands. How does this relate to your situation?

God, Surely You Blew It This Time!
Three Hebrew Boys

1. How do you relate to the three Hebrew boys?

2. Shadrach, Meshach and Abednego refused to bow their knee to King Nebuchadnezzar's demands, choosing instead to remain faithful to God. Even with this bold, public display of their faithfulness to God, He still allowed them to go into the furnace. What goes through your mind when you consider this? Do you feel like God let them down? Did God let you down?

3. Think about the proclamation the boys made to the king where they told him that they knew God was able to save them, but even if He didn't they'd still refuse to bow their knee to anyone else. When have you needed holy boldness like this? How did you respond?

4. When Nebuchadnezzar looked into the flames, he saw four men rather than three walking unhurt the fire. How does it encourage you to know that God walks with you through the fires of grief? How does it feel to know that God knew before time began that you would walk through the fires of miscarriage?

5. What would have happened if the young men stayed in the fire after God was ready to lead them out? Relate this to your grief. What will happen to your heart if you stay too long in the furnace of grief? What can you do to help yourself step out of the flames?

6. How have you dealt with anger following the death of your baby? Why is anger such a devastating emotion? How can you let the peace of Christ rule in you?

God, Surely You Blew It This Time!
Lazarus

1. How do you relate to Mary? Martha?

2. How do you think Mary and Martha felt when Jesus didn't show up when they thought He should? Has it felt like Jesus didn't show up when you needed Him?

3. How do you think this story would have been different if Jesus showed up before Lazarus died and He simply healed Him? What about if Lazarus died and Jesus never came?

4. How have you reconciled in your heart that God did not save your baby knowing that He had the ability to do so? Re-visit this thought with the story of Lazarus in mind. If you've not been able to do this yet, where are you in this journey?

5. Have you ever thought of Jesus crying when you hurt? How do you think Jesus feels about the loss of your baby? Get specific with what you envision Jesus doing, saying and feeling the day your baby died. How does it help you to know that Jesus grieves with you?

6. Take a few moments and envision the first moment your eyes see your child(ren) in eternity. Close your eyes and dream of what it really will be like. What do you see? Hear? Feel? Now envision seeing Jesus watching this reunion. What is He doing? Saying? Describe the look on His face.

God, Surely You Blew It This Time!
Calvary

1. Who do you most relate to in the account of Calvary? Confused disciples? Angry Peter? Devoted Mary?

2. Why do you think God's plan of Salvation included the death of His Baby? He could have chosen another plan for our redemption that didn't include the sacrifice of His Son. Why do you think He chose not to provide for our salvation another way?

3. How does it help you to know that God Himself grieved the death of His Child?

4. Imagine your baby fulfilling his/her part of God's plan without ever even drawing a breath. What does this mean to you? How does it feel to consider that your baby's life, no matter how brief, can bring glory to God?

5. Has your faith been shaken since your miscarriage? Is your faith now stronger or weaker? Now consider the grave. The grave no longer needs to be a reminder of the death of your baby, but a reminder of the resurrected life of your baby. Does this help rebuild your faith?

Weapons of Your Warfare

1. How do you relate to David?

2. Saul's armor was a poor fit for David. What poorly fitting armor have you worn in your battle to survive miscarriage? When did you realize that the armor was more harmful than helpful? After reading Ephesians 6, what part of the armor of God is easiest for you to take on? Which is the hardest?

3. What are your giants? Fear of another miscarriage? Disappointment with God? Marital problems? Depression? Which is the greatest? Make a list of all your giants, and then list a Name of God to defeat each one.

4. Goliath taunted the armies of Israel day after day. How has Satan taunted you since your loss?

5. Goliath fell forward! How have your giants fallen forward? How would you like to see them fall forward? If you could write your story from today forward, how would you want God to use your miscarriage for good?

Stupid Sheep

1. As you read Psalm 23, how do you relate to David? When you think about David's baby dying, what new insights do you gain regarding this passage?

2. How does it feel to know that you must *walk* through grief? How does it feel to know that you must walk *through* grief?

3. Have you gotten "stuck" in your grief? How do you know? What will it take for you to pull your feet out of the sand and continue on your journey?

4. Think about God being present with you as you grieve. How does it change how you grieve? When have you felt Him the most? How have you felt the comfort of His rod and staff?

5. Grief is a season of your life and not a lifelong assignment. What other seasons of your life can you identify?

6. Use the analogy of the rear view mirror to describe how devastating it is to always look backward. Are you looking backward too much? How does it feel when you consider moving forward from grief and letting this experience remain a part of your history?

Mary's Oil
An Unrecoverable Sacrifice

1. How can you relate to Mary?

2. Mary poured out her oil, which she could never replace, and Jesus accepted it as an offering of her love. How is your baby like this oil?

3. Jesus said Mary had done what she could. Have you condemned yourself for not doing more to save your baby or for being the cause of your miscarriage? How does Jesus' response to Mary's critics make you feel?

4. How does your brokenness need to be restored? How are you like the vessel the Potter wants to rebuild?

5. Have you poured your sorrow at the feet of Jesus? If so, how did it feel? If not, what stops you? Anger? Disappointment? Disbelief?

They Are Precious in His Sight
Psalm 139

1. Can you relate to David when he wrote Psalm 139?

2. Think about God being present with your baby in your womb. How does this change how you think and feel about the moment of your baby's death?

3. Your baby was created in the image and likeness of God Himself. How does it feel when you consider the preciousness of your baby to God?

4. Have you ever really considered that fact that your baby's life had meaning? Your baby accomplished something in God's plan that no one else could have. Discuss how you feel about this.

5. God knew before your baby was conceived that he or she would not survive the pregnancy. If God knew this child would never live outside of the womb, why do you think He allowed your baby to be conceived? Why didn't He refuse to allow this baby to be conceived, thus sparing you the sorrow of miscarriage? How does it comfort you to know that God has perfect wisdom?

6. How does the Christian grieve differently than the non-Christian? Why should a Christian have to grieve at all?

Appendix B

Encouraging Scriptures

❦

There can be no greater source of encouragement throughout any battle than the powerful Word of God. It has never failed. It will never fail. Any promise written on those holy pages is infallible. You can bank your life and your eternity on those words.

The following Scriptures are given as suggestions for you to meditate on as you deal with miscarriage and the struggle that it brings. There is also space provided for you to write down other Scriptures that are particularly encouraging to you personally. Psalm 119:105 tells us that the Word of God is a lamp unto our feet and a light unto our path. Sometimes your path may grow dim and you cannot see where to turn. Turn to Scripture. Proverbs 30:5 tells us that every word of God is tested; He is a shield to those who take refuge in Him. When you're hurting, don't run from God. Run to Him as hard and fast as you can. He'll become a shield around you.

Memorize these words. Write them on your heart. Keep the Word of God in front of you all the time. Why not write scriptures on business cards and tape them to your bathroom mirror? Every time you brush your teeth, there are God's promises staring you in the face! Place scriptures by the door of your home to remind you of God's provision and protection every time you enter or exit. Tuck verses away inside your wallet as a constant reminder each time you pull out a dollar bill or write a check. You will defeat Satan with the

151

Word. Make it an integral part of your battle to survive the heartache of miscarriage.

"Your word is a lamp to my feet and a light to my path." Psalm 119:105

"Trust in the LORD with all your heart and do not lean on your own understanding. In all your ways acknowledge Him, and He will make your paths straight." Proverbs 3:5-6

"The Light shines in the darkness, and the darkness did not comprehend it." John 1:5

"I am the Light of the world; he who follows Me will not walk in the darkness, but will have the Light of life." John 8:12

"'For I know the plans I have for you,' declares the LORD, 'plans to prosper you and not to harm you, plans to give you hope and a future.'" Jeremiah 29:11

"And He got up and rebuked the wind and said to the sea, "Hush, be still." And the wind died down and it became perfectly calm." Mark 4:35-39

"This is my comfort in my affliction, that Your word has revived me." Psalm 119:50

"Shout for joy, O heavens! And rejoice, O earth! Break forth into joyful shouting, O mountains! For the LORD has comforted His people and will have compassion on His afflicted." Isaiah 49:13

"Blessed be the God and Father of our Lord Jesus Christ, the Father of mercies and God of all comfort, who comforts us in all our affliction so that we will be able to comfort those who are in any affliction with the comfort with which we ourselves are comforted by God. For just as the sufferings of Christ are ours in abundance, so also our comfort is abundant through Christ." 2 Corinthians 1:3-5

"But we do not want you to be uninformed, brethren, about those who are asleep, so that you will not grieve as do the rest who have no hope." 1 Thessalonians 4:13

"Truly, truly, I say to you, that you will weep and lament, but the world will rejoice; you will grieve, but your grief will be turned into joy." John 16:20

"Because of the LORD's great love we are not consumed, for his compassions never fail. They are new every morning; great is your faithfulness." Lamentations 3:22-23

"The LORD your God, who is going before you, will fight for you, as he did for you in Egypt, before your very eyes," Deuteronomy 1:30

"Now faith is the assurance of things hoped for, the conviction of things not seen." Hebrews 11:1

"So the ransomed of the LORD will return and come with joyful shouting to Zion, and everlasting joy will be on their heads. They will obtain gladness and joy, and sorrow and sighing will flee away." Isaiah 51:11

"This is my comfort in my affliction, that Your word has revived me." Psalm 119:50

"...Do not be grieved, for the joy of the LORD is your strength." Nehemiah 8:10

"...but because Jesus lives forever, he has a permanent priesthood. Therefore he is able to save completely those who come to God through him, because he always lives to intercede for them." Hebrews 7:24-25 (NIV)

"Lo, I am with you always" (Matthew 28:20)

"...And they cried out in fear. [27]*But immediately Jesus spoke to them, saying, 'Take courage, it is I; do not be afraid.'"* Matthew 14:26-27

"Blessed be the God of Shadrach, Meshach and Abednego, who has sent His angel and delivered His servants who put their trust in Him," Daniel 3:28

"When you walk through the fire, you will not be burned; the flames will not set you ablaze. For I am the LORD, your God, the Holy One of Israel, your Savior." Isaiah 43:2b-3a

"I've come that they might have life and have it more abundantly." John 10:10

"You will seek Me and find Me when you search for Me with all your heart." Jeremiah 29:13

"Therefore, take up the full armor of God, so that you will be able to resist in the evil day, and having done everything, to stand firm." Ephesians 6:13

"O LORD, how my adversaries have increased! Many are rising up against me. Many are saying of my soul, 'There is no deliverance for him in God,' But You, O LORD, are a shield about me, My glory, and the One who lifts my head." Psalm 3:1-3

"To every thing there is a season, and a time to every purpose under the heaven: A time to be born, and a time to die; a time to plant, and a time to pluck up that which is planted; A time to kill, and a time to heal; a time to break down, and a time to build up; A time to weep, and a time to laugh; a time to mourn, and a time to dance;" Ecclesiastes 3:1-3 (KJV)

"Let the peace of Christ rule in your hearts". Colossians 3:15

She has done what she could. Mark 14:8

"For I am convinced that neither death nor life, neither angels nor demons, neither the present nor the future, nor any powers, neither height nor depth, nor anything else in all creation, will be able to separate us from the love of God that is in Christ Jesus our Lord." Romans 8:38

"The Lord is close to the brokenhearted and saves those who are crushed in spirit." Psalm 34:18

"He heals the brokenhearted and binds up their wounds." Psalm 147:3

"A broken and contrite heart, O God, you will not despise." Psalm 51:17

"He who formed you says do not fear. I've called you by name." Isaiah 43:1

"The LORD is my shepherd, I shall not want. He makes me lie down in green pastures; He leads me beside quiet waters. He restores my soul; He guides me in the paths of righteousness for His name's sake. Even though I walk through the valley of the shadow of death I fear no evil, for You are with me; Your rod and Your staff, they comfort me. You prepare a table before me in the presence of my enemies; You have anointed my head with oil; my cup overflows. Surely goodness and lovingkindness will follow me all the days of my life, and I will dwell in the house of the LORD forever." Psalm 23:1-6

Other scriptures encouraging to me:

_____

_____

_____

_____

Appendix C

Sarah's Laughter

Christian Support for Infertility & Child Loss

❧❧

S arah's Laughter is a ministry dedicated to healing the hurts of those struggling with infertility or the death of a baby to miscarriage or stillbirth. Whether suffering from the loss of a child or the loss of the dream of the family one may never have, the pain of childlessness is overwhelming. Throughout Scripture we see people just like you and me who have, on bended knee, pleaded with God for the life of a child, both born and unborn. There is so much we can glean from these precious, sacred words to heal the hurt and give encouragement that the world simply cannot give.

Using Scripture as a guide, Sarah's Laughter reaches out to those living with the burden of infertility and miscarriage and guides them through this quagmire of depression and desperation with a rock solid biblical foundation based on God's love and plan for each of us. Through conferences and workshops, hurting people are given hope that God understands their pain and is constantly working on their behalf. Pastors and loved ones find tangible gifts to give to bereaved parents grieving the loss of a baby with miscarriage gifts available through this ministry. Through God's provision, we have

been blessed to open the *Sarah's Laughter Center for Infertility &
Miscarriage Support*, offering support and encouragement in Baton
Rouge, Louisiana. For those unable to visit the center, our website
provides 24-hour support and offers a place where hurting people
can find encouragement anytime of the day or night.

If you have any questions regarding this ministry or if you know
of a couple who could benefit, please do not hesitate to contact us at
any time. We will be more than happy to work with you as we serve
together as vessels for the Master's use.

Beth Forbus, MA
Founder
Sarah's Laughter
Christian Support for Infertility & Child Loss
www.Sarahs-Laughter.com

Appendix D

Baby Hunger
Biblical Encouragement for Those Struggling with Infertility

By

Beth Forbus

***B**aby Hunger* gives a scholarly look at the Scripture as it relates to infertility, personal loss, and the ability to put your life in God's hands with the absolute knowledge that He is always in total control. When I read Baby Hunger, I was amazed! There are a lot of books out there about infertility, but this one touched me. As I read it, it even touched me in the loss of my mother. There's nothing like *Baby Hunger*. You can't find anything else like it. Get this book!

Dr. Bobby W. Webster, Medical Director,
A Woman's Center for Reproductive Medicine, Baton Rouge, Louisiana

Baby Hunger is available on-line at www.Sarahs-Laughter.com, Amazon.com, BarnesandNoble.com or XulonPress.com. It may also be ordered through your local bookstore.